# Baseball Fathers, Baseball Sons

# Baseball Fathers, Baseball Sons

# DICK WIMMER

William Morrow and Company, Inc.
New York

**Library of Congress Cataloging-in-Publication Data**

Wimmer, Dick.
    Baseball fathers, baseball sons.
    1. Baseball players—United States—Biography.
    2. Fathers and sons—United States—Case studies.
    I. Title.
GV865.A1W68    1988        796.357′092′2 [B]    87-34880
ISBN 0-688-07634-3

Printed in the United States of America

First Edition

1 2 3 4 5 6 7 8 9 10

BOOK DESIGN BY PHIL REDISCH

# Acknowledgments

I am indebted to the following major league publicity directors for their help and cooperation: Steve Brener of the Dodgers, and his assistant, Ruth Ruiz; Dick Bresciani of the Red Sox; Larry Shenk of the Phillies; Jim Toomey of the Cardinals; Sharon Pannozzo of the Cubs; Tim Mead and John Sevano of the Angels; Dean Vogelaar of the Royals; Bob Brown of the Orioles; Harvey Greene of the Yankees; Jay Horwitz of the Mets; and Dan Ewald of the Tigers.

I would also like to thank my editor, Adrian Zackheim, and his assistant, Pam Altschul, for their encouragement; the enigmatic Paul Wagner for his wisdom; and finally, the players themselves, and their fathers and sons.

# Baseball Fathers, Baseball Sons

# Chapter One

All morning I kept recalling my father and me on those bright, windy Saturdays when I was twelve, journeying up to the Stadium together and across the terrifying catwalks behind his impatient, slope-shouldered stride, "Come on, come on, nothing to be scared of up here," to watch far below the groundskeepers hose down the diamond, the pitchers slowly getting loose, kids scampering along the aisles in pursuit of batting practice homers that bounced high off the silver railings as we eagerly waited for Williams to appear, Raschi meeting with Rizzuto at the mound, the Yankee infield and out-field shifting way around to the right, and Ted, tapping the dirt from his spikes and twisting the bat in his hands, nervously digging into place with that tall, classic stance, our raccoon eyes squinting and my father smiling and nudging me with a whisper, "This is some game, huh? Glad I took you? Huh? You've got some father. You'll see, just wait'll you have a son of your own."

And now here in California, nearly forty years later, I have two—a single parent for close to a decade—with the constant link of baseball between us since they could walk, playing and coaching and retelling tales of my boyhood heroes and discovering all of their new ones as suddenly, in the wink of an eye, they're both in their teens and the rebellion that's been looming has, in fact, already begun.

But enough of that now, since I have got to get dressed, quickly fitting on my brown baseball cap with the yellow "C" and matching warm-up jacket, then hustling out to my car under a clear blue California sky for the fifteen-minute ride to Calabasas High School. We're halfway through a season of eighteen games in this, my first spring of coaching the JV, and my fourteen-year-old son Geordie, as we take on our archrivals, Agoura, today, while on the adjacent diamond, his older brother, Ceo (pronounced Kee-O), seventeen, will be in center field and batting third for the varsity.

Traffic, to my surprise, is lighter than usual for a Tuesday afternoon as I breeze along, and my thoughts keep returning once more to Ted Williams and our extraordinary meeting with him almost a year ago last March:

"I can't believe we're really going, Dad, I thought you were just joking when you first talked about it!" Geordie chattered on excitedly as the three of us strapped ourselves aboard the Northwest Orient flight from L.A. to Tampa during spring break and zoomed away across the country, our conversation glittering with the magic names of Boggs and Mattingly, Ozzie and Schmidt, Hershiser and Cal Ripken, Jr.—for those were only a few of the current players we were off to meet and talk to on that once-in-a-lifetime trip, while I reminisced with such stars of my era as Stan the Man Musial, Sandy Koufax, Joe DiMaggio, and my all-time hero, Ted Williams, The Thumper, The Splendid Splinter, Teddy Ballgame, about their fathers and their sons.

Since many of the old-timers served solely as batting or pitching instructors during the Grapefruit League and spring training camps of Florida, we knew this was probably our best opportunity to catch them all together in one convenient spot. Come summer, the three of us would set off again, from L.A. to Boston and back, stopping in various major league cities to take in a game and, afterward, interview more of our favorite stars from the present and the past.

But then, on that day, March 22, 1986, as across the country we flew, Geordie, the ultimate baseball fan, was still leaning forward on the edge of his seat, calling it "a kid's fantasy come true," his lank brown hair brushed smoothly in place, the face of my father scrubbed shiny and clean, statistics tingling from his fingertips (give him an average, any average, for last season and he'd tell you his name: ".282?" "Easy, Cal Ripken, Jr." ".276?" "Ozzie Smith"), zealous reader of *Sports Illustrated* and *The Sporting News,* collector of mountainous stacks of baseball cards, avid player of Strat-O-Matic, watcher of ESPN's *Sports Center,* and All-Star pitcher and shortstop on his Little League team, while Ceo, three years older, blond and blue-eyed and strappingly healthy at six feet, 175, with the look of a California surfer (who loved to play ball, but couldn't care less about stats and rarely watched TV games), kept telling him to shut up and "Stop acting like a Lame-o!" as I smiled beside them on the aisle, wearing my Red Sox cap, of course, a dark blue windbreaker—

And soon we were landing, coming down over nighttime Tampa Bay with that strange feeling of a city first seen—wanting it to look different—and in a way it was, with an occasional "You all" drawl and Uncle Tom's Barbeque Chips (no sign of ballplayers sprawled about in civvies or clicking cleats across the lounge), but our Avis Chevy was ready with a full tank of gas and off we roared into the balmy southern air.

At 6:30 the next morning, we were out of our motel and shooting up Route 4 to the lazy little town of Winter Haven, Florida, and Chain O'Lakes Park, home of the Boston Red Sox. There were several diamonds—minor league fields, we assumed—spread down to the right, and no one on them, as we turned left and headed toward the clubhouse for a prearranged meeting with Ted Williams. I didn't know what to expect: Would he be gruff and acerbic, dismissing me with a rude rebuff as he'd done with so many writers in the past?

We pulled to a stop by the empty press room lounge and ran into Dick Bresciani, the friendly PR man, who was leaving for Fort Myers and a B game against the Royals. He told us that Williams should be here soon, "Nine, nine-thirty, he usually gets in, but you never know, 'cause John Henry, his son's here, too."

Geordie watched in awe as Marty Barrett and Dwight Evans strolled by, and then—with a deep breath and a running start—asked for their autographs, and one from the dour Jim Rice (when he was Geordie's age, he'd been a starter for his American Legion team), who strode silently, massively past, didn't even acknowledge the request till he reached his locker, then turned, and muttered, "C'mere," and swiftly scrawled his name. This same Jim Rice, who once hit sixteen consecutive pitches out of Fenway during batting practice, alone before his locker, and my sons and I in the Red Sox clubhouse, no other reporters in sight—for the team had finished 18½ games out the year before (and no one could conceive then of Clemens' Cy Young and the postseason wonders to come)—and no sign of Williams as yet. Only a white golf cart that he alone used. The three of us walking out toward the diamond with the dark green carpet of outfield grass shimmering in the sun, then springy under our feet—surprised how sharply it sloped away from the rim of the infield—as the boys went racing across it, imagining themselves making that great over-the-shoulder, leaping one-hand catch in deep left center. And my own fantasy that Williams would arrive and ask me to hit, and go crazy at this "Natural's" grace and bat speed as I put out that tall bank of lights, call for McNamara, and "Roy Hobbs" Wimmer will sign a contract right there on the spot!

The sun kept blazing down and still no Williams as, amazingly, we sat alone in the Red Sox dugout and watched Wade Boggs take batting practice. Ceo marveling at his smooth stroke, with more players appearing, starters and rookies we'd never seen, Roger Clemens saying hello, and Geordie detailing Boggs' stats last year, ".368, .351 lifetime, only popped out twice—" as he kept lacing line drives into left, center, and right.

At nine-thirty we moved back to the clubhouse with

the news that Williams had arrived, was inside, and would be out in a moment. We hurried along, all those boyhood images of my father and me suddenly whirling through my mind.

*And there he was!* The Splendid Splinter, Teddy Ballgame, the best, no question about it, that I've ever seen—now sixty-seven years old but still Williams as he came urgently striding out, beefy round the middle and leathery, weather-beaten handsome at an imposing six-four, with his Red Sox cap, sunglasses, white warm-up jacket, sports shirt, and slacks—and intercepted by me.

"What's this about?" as he continued walking toward the field. "Baseball fathers and baseball sons, Dick Bresciani—" "Well how long'll it take?" "Just a few minutes—" "Awright, well then let's get it over with, don't take too long now." Oh my God, a vision of having just flown three thousand miles for a two-minute interview!

We sat along the right-field line, with the boys before us taking snapshots, and I had to keep blinking and swallowing hard to believe I was finally sitting beside Ted Williams. He'd been my hero so long as I regaled my sons with his prowess that now their love of me had passed through him, whom they'd never seen play, and he'd become their hero, too.

And far from the bristling legend I'd expected, I found a warm and generous man, with great bursts of enthusiasm, quick and bright—who ultimately made me feel as though I were talking to my father (or possibly through my father) in a frozen moment of time.

"Did your father ever play sports?"

"No, he joined the Army early, he got in the cavalry, and he really didn't participate in sports too much."

"Did he encourage you in baseball?"

"Well not as much as you'd think. Really, he never became interested in what I was doin' athletically at all until he saw my name in the paper on the high school team, and all of a sudden, why, I'd pitched a good game or I'd hit a good ball and then he started to pay a little attention my last year. His great interest was, of course, on Saturday, when we'd play a game. This is really kinda funny. On Saturday when we'd play a game, why, he'd always make sure I'd have a steak about twelve o'clock. Well, gee, I was out there one-thirty with a steak and, you know, his intentions were good, but I'm not sure he helped me too much with that timing!"

"Did it bring you closer together?"

"Yes, I'd say so, after I started playing professional. Though I was in the East and he was in the West and he never saw me play very much; I'm not even sure with television he saw me play very much."

"How'd you feel about that?"

"Well, you know, I look back on my life and I was so completely involved with what I was doin', playin' baseball and tryin' to get ahead and tryin' to save money, tryin' to get life insurance and helpin' my mother and father, and hunting and fishing, that that was it."

"What about your relationship with your son?"

"Well I hope it's closer than I ever was with my father.

Not that I didn't love my father, but I've had more time to be with John Henry, despite the fact that I don't get to see him as much as I'd like. But I certainly watch every detail of his life and I am conscious of how important education is. I wasn't very well educated, and that's really my biggest concern, that he's going to get a red-hot education."

"Did you encourage him in sports in any way?"

"O you bet I do. And he's interested in sports, and, of course, knowin' his dad was in sports, why, he's got a little more of that interest goin' to start with, see, than I did."

"But how do you follow a legend?"

"Well I'm not so keen as to how closely he follows my career in baseball. I'm more concerned at this point that he get the best possible education that I can possibly get for him and he takes advantage of it, and I'll take my chances from then on with him."

"How old is he?"

"Well he's seventeen years old. He's goin' to Vermont Academy and he's already been accepted to Bates, which is a very fine school up in Maine, and so I'm happy about that."

"What would you have done if you hadn't played ball?"

"I don't know. I would've been in the laps of the gods, I guess, I don't know. There's a chance that after I got into the service and after I started to fly and I had nothing to go back to, I might've considered staying in the service. Because there were things about flying that

I liked and it was probably the biggest accomplishment that I've ever made, becoming a naval aviator, a Marine pilot, and so I might've pursued that, I don't know."

"Has the adjustment been hard once baseball was over?"

"Not a bit. Heck sake, I played till I knew that I didn't wanna play anymore, that was over with, out. And I been very fortunate in what's happened to me since I got outta baseball in a lotta ways."

"Why do you think so few sons have followed their fathers into baseball?"

"Well it's a hard act to follow, and I think it's harder today for *any* kid to excel in sports as well as their fathers did. Because I don't think they have the time, they're lookin' at television, they're gonna have other interests, and all the major sports are involved now. But when I was a kid, it was baseball, baseball, baseball, baseball. So it's harder for a kid, and surprisingly, you can't name too many kids that've come up behind their fathers."

"How would you like to be remembered as a father?"

"Well I'd like my kid to say, 'Boy, my dad was a helluva guy and he loved me and he did everything he could for me and he gimme the right advice and he was an extra-special guy.' Bye-bye!"

And he was briskly off with another burst of nervous energy to coach the minor league hitters, giving Ceo his autograph and signing a ball for Geordie—Carl Yastrzemski behind him in the shadows—when he abruptly spun around and yelled back at me, "Now there's the guy you wanna talk to, he's gotta kid comin' up in Triple-A, talk to him, talk to him!"

And so I did, as Williams went striding away through blazing sunshine. Yaz, I was surprised to find, was roughly my height, with a slight paunch and graying hair, but intense as ever and still ready, I imagined, to take over in a pinch. He'd grown up in the small farming community of Bridgehampton, Long Island, not too distant, though miles away in lifestyle, from where I was raised in affluent, suburban Great Neck. I'd read his autobiography, remembering how he and his father had played on the same semipro team together, batting third and fourth, and that he seemed to be in large measure fulfilling his father's dream. I'd seen him play in person only once, during his rookie season of 1961, on my lone trip to Fenway, when the fans would cheer his splendid running catch in the corner one inning, then boo him unmercifully the next for popping out to short (he hardly pulled in those days; most of his hits were sliced late to left).

"How encouraging was your father when you were growing up?"

"Well he used to work with me every day. But, also, there was a much simpler lifestyle then, where there was more time involved, comin' from Long Island. He worked on a farm from six in the mornin' till six at night, then we had that two-two and a half hours to work out with me every night. I could work out with a semipro team that he played with, and you were constantly playing baseball, seven days a week. There was no extra activity such as boating and different things like that. It was just baseball, baseball, baseball."

"And his dream was to be a major leaguer?"

"Well he hurt his arm when he was young. He coulda signed with the Dodgers and the Cardinals, he had plenty of opportunity, but he figured that he just wouldn't make it to the big leagues account of the arm."

"One time near the end of your career, you said baseball was never fun, it was always hard work. Were you misquoted?"

"Well it was fun hittin' the ball and everything else, but to get to where it's fun, it was a tremendous amount of hard physical and mental work. Especially for me. I was never six-three, six-four. I was six foot, 180 pounds, I didn't have the leverage, the height, the strength that a lot of people had to do things with when you made a mistake. Everything with me had to be perfect. I had to have the hips, the arms, everything goin' together, so I thought I was a little at a disadvantage. The one thing that I wished I *was* was six-three, six-four and 210 pounds, then I'm sure it'd been much more fun."

"Did you ever feel you were fulfilling your father's dream by becoming the player that he could've been?"

"No, you had your own dream and that's what you worked for. That's one of the reasons down here I have it set that my kids, the minor leaguers that I work with hitting, they have to be dressed, they have to be down in the cage at eight-fifteen, even though the workouts don't start till ten o'clock. You wanna make it in the big leagues, it's gonna take a lot of hard work, being regimented, being on a strict schedule, and showin' 'em that this is what you have to do to get there."

"What would you have done if you hadn't been a ballplayer?"

"I don't know, I really don't know. There was never any doubt in my mind that I wasn't goin' to be a ballplayer. I just had that much confidence in myself. I did so much more than the next guy, and that's what it comes down to, the guy who does the extra work, concentrates harder mentally, he's the guy that makes it."

"You think if you'd come up today with the bonuses, the big money, it would've changed your life at all?"

"No, no, once you're on that field, there's only one thing on your mind and that is to be the *best*, be the best you can. Yeah, maybe over the wintertime you talk contracts and money and stuff like that, but once you get on the field, it's pride, it's all pride."

"Your son is now in the minor leagues. Is it hard for him to follow a legend?"

"I don't know. I talked to him a little about it. I know the fans get on him and stuff like that, it doesn't seem to bother him, but he has a tougher road to go through 'cause of the pressure on him than say just a Joe Blow, who was signed to the minor leagues, 'cause of the name factor. But I went through the same thing when I joined the Red Sox. I was takin' Ted Williams' place, every move I made was compared to Ted Williams, so there's no doubt about it, there is added pressure."

"How would you like to be remembered as a father?"

"How would I like to be remembered as a father? That's some question, y'know?" and he laughed, looking out at the batting practice before him. "There again you miss most of the things as your kids grow up, the high school plays, different things like that, but I still say a majority of the fathers who travel and work are in the same situation, so it's not like it was forty years ago or thirty-five years ago when I was growin' up, when you had fathers around every single second, every single day."

"Are you happy that your son's a ballplayer? Would it've mattered to you?"

"No, it wouldn't've mattered to me. As long as he's happy. He wants to give it a shot, he wants to try it, that's his decision."

"Is he your only son?"

"He's my only son, I have three daughters, right. But he's a good student, he's majoring in accounting and finance in college, he has another semester to go, which he'll finish up this year. So by taking the shot, he's never gonna have any regrets, 'Well I wish I had taken it,' instead of not taking it."

"Finally, did you ever consider, even for a moment, becoming a farmer like your father?"

"The only thing there was no doubt in my mind about was that I was goin' to play major league baseball. I knew I'd be in the major leagues, I just knew it."

We then shook hands, he gave the boys his autograph, and, as I watched him take off behind Williams to work with the minor leaguers, I couldn't help thinking of those lines from Pete Gammons' fine book *Beyond the Sixth Game,* describing Yaz as a "WPA figure with a foreboding personality who doggedly went about his job with a hard, competitive drive. He became, like his countryman Pope, whom he idolized, a symbol of the workingman on the throne of stardom—the average Joe who worked for everything he got."

Geordie was still staring in awe at the ball Williams had signed and quoting, " 'To Geordie, your pal, Ted Williams.' That's *rad,* Dad, rad!" when one of the reporters whispered that the tall, dark, and Hollywood-handsome boy passing by in a Red Sox uniform with a big blue 9 on the back and wearing two batting gloves was Ted's son, John Henry. I introduced myself and Ceo and Geordie, told him of the project, and we moved into the press room, where the four of us sat alone, Ceo snapping pictures and John Henry very composed.

"Did your father encourage you as a baseball player?"

"Well I can remember when I was real young, six or so, he used to throw a tennis ball at me and I'd hit it with a tennis racket. But he never really forced it or anything. I just always liked the game, I always liked baseball."

"Was he critical of you in any way?"

"No, he'd just let me swing. And after a while, he gave me a bat, but he'd still throw the tennis ball. And if the ball came right at me, I'd let it hit me, you know, I wouldn't move, it'd just bounce off me. And he'd say, 'Well you'd better get out of the way of 'em.' But I never did, 'cause it didn't hurt whenever it hit me, and I'd just keep on swinging."

"Did it bring you closer together?"

"I don't think so, no, not really. I never did see him much when I was younger, not till I was twelve, thirteen."

"Do you play baseball now?"

"Yes. I play first base. And I love it, it's my favorite sport."

"Is it hard being the son of a legend?"

"It is, they expect me to do a lot more. I mean, I may surprise 'em sometimes, but they're always saying, 'Gee, he struck out,' you know? And it's always, when-ever I get up, no matter who we're playing, the other coach just knows who I am, and for some reason he'll just move back his outfield—and they've never even seen me hit before!"

"Has your father seen you play?"

"No, he hasn't. He's going to, though, this year he said he would."

"Have you missed that?"

"Not really. I'm happy. I'd like him to come up to Bates this year, be good."

"What were you praised for as a child by him?"

"Being a good boy and having good manners."

"But not sports?"

"No."

"Do you see yourself becoming a major leaguer?"

"Not really, not yet."

"Would you like to be?"

"I don't know, half and half, maybe. It would be nice, but I have to worry about college right now."

"Do you have any other ambitions?"

"My dad wants me to work hard with business. And after I get a business background, then I could do whatever I want."

"When I say, 'Your father,' what's the first thing that comes to mind, the first image?"

John Henry considered this a moment before stretching his hands high, then out to the sides, and we all laughed together.

"Big and wide, huh?"

And smiling, he nodded and looked away.

"Has it been hard to get to know him because he's older, was fifty when you were born?"

"Well, it sometimes is. You know, he's back with tradition, he's back in his day. I mean it seems weird, but he doesn't look sixty-seven and he doesn't really act sixty-seven, but sometimes he'll say something and he'll want me to do something, and he has a very strong will about him."

"Ron Fairly, who knows your dad quite well, and

whose son plays on Ceo's high school team, said to me before we left on this trip that 'He's the most dominant human being you'll ever meet. If he walked into a room of presidents and kings, he'd be the center of attention.' "

"That's right, he wouldn't care, he'd act the same way."

"I guess that could be a little scary for a son?"

"I get embarrassed sometimes—I mean sometimes."

"But he's also very warm, very giving."

"Yeah, he is."

"Does he let you hit here?"

"He's gonna throw to me in a few minutes, so I'd better get going."

"Do you mind if we tag along?"

"No, not at all."

And we all headed down to the minor league fields as John Henry, shy yet composed, moved into a long, net-enclosed batting cage where his father sat on a bucket behind a small protective screen, former Red Sox first baseman George Scott beside him, and softly tossed up ball after ball to his tall, good-looking son, who took a wide-open, right-handed stance.

"What'd you do that time?" Williams asked, following a swing and a miss, and tossing up another ball.

"I missed it."

Still tossing, "Hips in front of hands."

And John Henry, lean and tense like a high-strung horse now, kept swinging and soon began lining the ball, often as not, off the sides of the cage or over his father's head. And the touching thing to me was how kind, considerate, and understanding Williams was to his son: gentle, prodding, never harsh, always supportive, and backing off when he touched a nerve.

John Henry abruptly asking, "What about my ankle? I keep twisting my ankle when I swing."

"It's OK, it's OK."

"No, it's *not* OK, that shouldn't be!"

John Henry switching to the left side then as Ted came out of the cage, "He'll see many more right-handers in college," and George Scott began flipping up the balls. Williams standing next to me, both of us wearing our flapping windbreakers, and I thought how hard it was to follow a legend—or rather impossible—to establish who you are. The struggle of all sons? To some degree. To break free and become yourself, realizing as I had over these years that all sons are separate, almost strangers, and should be seen as such, not merely our flesh and blood; and the two basic things we can teach them in life are first to walk and then to walk away.

Suddenly Williams grabbed me round the shoulders in a hearty grip and shouted, "Hey, here's a guy who knows baseball! When did you start watching?"

"Uh, 1946."

"And who does John Henry remind you of?"

"The first hitter that comes to mind? Don Demeter."

"Well that could be, that could be, but I never really saw him, he was in the other league. But who else? Back then, huh, who else?"

And, of course, I knew the name he wanted—the best ballplayer he'd ever seen.

"Joe DiMaggio."

"See, see!" Ted smiling at Scott, "Didn't I tell you? The same wide stance and hips cocked—that's right, exactly right!"

When John Henry was through, I asked if Ceo could follow him in, and unbelievably Williams agreed: John Henry taking over the "pitching" from behind the BP screen as all of us watched, along with a handful of fans and passing minor leaguers, Ceo in his gray shorts and striped, light blue sports shirt, sneakers and high white socks. But before he began, Williams just had him swing the bat in the cage, no pitching, "Just your normal swing."

And as soon as he did, out came a flurry of rapid comments: "He's hitting down, he's hitting down. Drop your hands, drop your hands. More, more! You're looking at the plate. Look out there, follow the ball. Your hips're going one way and your head another. Hips in front of hands, face the way you wanna hit the ball, hips in front of hands!"

And soon thereafter, left-handed-hitting Ceo began whacking line drives off every part of the cage.

"There! Now he's got it, now he's got it!" Williams whirling around, facing me, and asking, "Where's his head, following the ball, hips in front of hands?"

"Right."

"See, see!"

And for the next thirty minutes, my son hit under

the watchful eye of Ted Williams as John Henry kept pitching and Ceo kept ripping shot after shot with that smooth, powerful swing, head down, hips in front of hands, and Williams leaned toward me, "He's a strong kid. How old is he?"

"Sixteen."

"*Sixteen?* He's good, he's good, just keep that head up and follow the ball."

George Scott asking, "He on a team?"

"Yeah, in Calabasas, California."

Williams leaning toward me again. "And *how* old is he?"

"Sixteen."

"When'll he be seventeen?"

"August."

"August what?"

"Twenty-fifth."

Williams grinned. "John Henry's on the twenty-sixth!"

Now all the balls were used up as Ceo and John Henry emerged together, Williams and I walking away side by side, and he said, "That'll be a hundred dollars the half hour."

I laughed, "You kidding? You can name your price!"

I asked Geordie if he wanted a turn, but he begged off, shy in the shadow of his brother, afraid to compete, to fail or disappoint: And how much more could I ask of Williams as he hopped in the golfing cart with his son and sped away, at sixty-seven still brimming with life, or rather striding through it, just like he hit, never at rest, twisting impatient hands about the bat. And the three of us wishing we could've seen *him* swing. But all we were allowed were those rare moments when he'd reveal a stunning flash of that powerful grace that filled me again with wonder and memory of that tall classic stance, nervously digging into place.

On our way back to our car, we bumped into Wade Boggs, dressed after practice in a striped T-shirt and Bermuda shorts, who kindly granted us an interview, alone again in the press room. There, across the table from me, sat Ceo's current hero at six-two with his fierce tunnel vision, bushy brown moustache, and soft voice as I recalled a smattering of facts about him: that he'd been an honor student in high school, an all-state punter, and been offered two scholarships to the University of South Carolina; that his father was a retired master sergeant in the Air Force and his mother (tragically killed in a car accident that June) was a pilot; that he had an intense love of chicken, which he ate every day, resulting in *Fowl Tips,* a chicken cookbook he and wife, Debbie (his high school sweetheart), wrote two years ago; that they had a daughter, Meagann, who was seven (and the following season, an infant son, Brett—named after his buddy, George, of the Royals—who was immediately put on a chicken formula); and finally, that Williams had said Boggs had the best hand-eye coordination of anyone he'd ever seen.

"Did your father play sports?"

"He played fast-pitch softball for twenty-five years in the service."

"Did he encourage you in any way?"

"He never pushed me. He just let me take it up and enjoy it. He managed me when I was in Little League and Senior League."

"Was he critical of you at all?"

"No, not at all. Just teaching the right instructions and, like I said, not pressing me about anything."

"Did it bring you closer together?"

"Oh, yeah. He would work with me, you know, from a coaching standpoint rather than a father standpoint, and that probably made it a little easier."

"Well it's funny, I've coached my kids, and as a friend of mine just said, 'It's enough your being their father without having to be their coach, too.' You think that applies to you?"

"Well a father's not going to yell at other kids on the team like he would a son. But if the father can take the attitude of teaching without yelling and making an example in front of other kids just because it's his son, then I don't think anything bad's been accomplished."

"Did your mother take an interest?"

"Oh, yeah, she'd go to Little League games and go to high school games and watch me play all the time."

"What were you praised for as a child?"

"Just obedience, never gettin' into trouble, and good manners, that kind of thing."

"Has your father followed your career, has he come up to Boston?"

"Oh, yeah, and we discuss various things about hitting. He was the one that I had to fall back on in the minor leagues, got my hitting instruction from, and he's still critical nowadays. As he says, he doesn't worry about the hits, he worries about the outs."

"What haven't you got in life by being a ballplayer? Any regrets?"

"Oh, no, I have none at all. I've always wanted to be a professional ballplayer on the major league level since the time I was six, and that's the only thing I've dedicated my life to be—and here I am."

"Has it been a strain on your family life?"

"No, not at all. My family loves it and everyone's getting out of it what's been expected."

"If you hadn't played ball, what would you have done?"

"Something in the athletic field, whether it be professional football or whatever I would put my mind to do. I had a lot of ability as a child in different areas—when I was five, I was able to hit off Little League pitchers who were nine, ten, and eleven years old—and it was just all I've ever wanted to do."

"How do you feel about your daughter playing sports?"

"Well she's taking up tennis and I've tried to get her into golf, see how she likes it."

"One last question: Has Williams been any help with your hitting?"

"Not really. We have Walt Hriniak, our hitting coach.

But I read Williams' book from cover to cover when I was in high school and it helped me then."

Something must have helped him, I thought, smiling to myself, for in his last eleven varsity games, Boggs hit at a .788 pace!

It was already noon now and we were due at one at Al Lang Field in St. Petersburg, where Stan Musial awaited. So we left lazy, laid-back Winter Haven, heading down Route 4 with Geordie still staring in awe at the ball Williams had signed, Ceo delighted that he'd said "Most of the things you said, Dad," "Well I also read his book," and me not quite believing as yet as we flashed past the orange groves that I'd just met this legend of my youth, who, more than fifty years ago, at Hoover High in San Diego, carried his bat to class, his glove hooked to his belt.

# Chapter Two

**B**ack in Calabasas, I swing into the staff parking lot, gather together my scorebook and clipboard, and begin the slow hike up the steep slope above the school, by the football field to the broad plateau of the varsity diamond, with its wire backstop and right-field fence some 330 feet away stretching off toward the open expanse of left center and left.

Ceo isn't there as yet. But Geordie is, as I continue along the foul line and up the short rise to the JV diamond, he and several of his teammates already seated in the dugout, snatches of their conversation drifting across:

"Where'd you kiss her?"

"On the lips."

"You lie!"

"How much, how much? I bet you ten thou!"

"She's a Shamu!"

"No way Boggs is better'n Mattingly? Mattingly's awesome, thirty-one homers, Gold Glove. . . ."

Geordie wincing and grimacing now as he shuffles toward me. "Can't throw, Dad, my arm's been killing me all morning."

"You want to sit this one out?"

"Nah, nah, I'll play."

And smiling, I shake my head at this standard routine, and he begins tossing a ball back and forth before finally jogging out to short with what he's sure is a "cool" major league swagger.

# Chapter Three

**A**l Lang Field that day offered baseball the way it should be played—on grass, at a leisurely pace, in a bandbox stadium with a great view of sea gulls and pelicans swooping and gliding over Tampa Bay—rather than what baseball's now sadly become: Astroturf and jai-lai bounces, computerized scoreboards replete with Diamondvision and TV commercials, jets screeching overhead, penthouse suites, and the fans far removed from the action.

Up to the press box we went, to be greeted by the Ed Wynnish-looking Cardinals' PR man Jim Toomey and the word that "Stan'll talk to you up here, and you can see Ozzie after the game." We took seats between reporters and their Radio Shack computers, the boys excited about rubbing elbows with the press from this "rad" vantage point, Geordie filling in what had just occurred on the field to a Montreal scribe who returned from the bathroom, and grinning back at me at being "part of the scene" as we watched St. Louis battle the Expos below and a kaleidoscope of images in the Florida sunshine: the Cardinals' wonderful logo that I've always loved of those two red birds perched on a yellow bat; John Tudor's compact windup and precise delivery, as though he were flicking darts in an English pub; Willie

McGee's seesawing running style, flipperlike heels flopping behind him as he whisked into second with a breezy steal; Tim Raines flinging his glove high in the air in left field after a controversial call, and being given the old heave-ho from this Grapefruit League game; pitchers jogging in small groups around the warning track while play was in progress; an old black vendor shouting, "Ice cold hot dogs!" before breaking into song, a raspy, bellowing version of "He's Got the Whole World in His Hands" and "Born in the U.S.A.," to enthusiastic applause; the Montreal writers leafing through their French dictionaries or talking over the numerous phones tied into other sports centers and baseball parks, shutting out the world, Libya, Qaddafi, and those "war games" taking place in the Gulf of Sidra; and the host of blue-rinsed, white-haired ladies escorted by the aged, courtly ushers—so serene it was a *Twilight Zone* scene and Sunday picnic atmosphere amid the stately southern drawls.

Later, I sat in an empty press box with Stan the Man, now sixty-five and a grandfather of eight. His engaging smile, easy, edgy grace, and surprisingly small hands led me to recall the finest description of him I've ever read in a nearly all but forgotten and long out-of-print novel, *Diary of a Simple Man,* by Peter Cohen:

> **Standing there with his feet together, his shoulders hunched and the bat almost straight up, he looked almost awkward, and then Branca gave him the low outside fastball. Musial took**

that sudden step, uncoiling like a spring, and
then the bat went around in a long sweep and
there was the crack that you never hear without
wanting to stand up, one fast look at Reese
leaping straddle-legged for the ball, and then the
ball was over the grass and then bouncing fast
between Reiser and Hermanski, Hermanski
lumbering slowly along the base of the wall and
Reiser running at an angle to play the carom,
taking it on the fly and throwing hard and low to
Stanky at second, Musial going in with a casual
slide, Jocko Conlan leaning down at the dust and
then jabbing both arms out low at his sides.

How many times had my father and I seen him over
the years at Ebbets Field and the Polo Grounds, or years
later in California, long after my father had died, going
to an Old Timers' Game at Dodger Stadium with my
sons and, as "The Man" wriggled once more into that
stance, "shoulders hunched and the bat almost straight
up," the tears suddenly filled my eyes—and I couldn't
stop crying—as "the bat went around in a long sweep
and there was the crack that you never hear without
wanting to stand up," and a line shot soaring out to deep
right field again.

"Did your father play sports?"

"No, he didn't play any sports, he came from Poland,
but he was interested in gymnastics and he got me interested in that; I used to drill and go to these various

meets, tumble and work on the horse and the parallel bars, so it was good training, because it taught you co-ordination and balance."

"So baseball was really foreign to him?"

"Well he knew about baseball, he always talked about Babe Ruth—of course, this was back in the thirties—and when I played sports in high school, he attended every game."

"Was he critical of you in any way?"

"Well he wanted me to go to college, and I had a scholarship to go to Pitt in basketball at the same time I got the Cardinal offer. But I had a hard time convincing him that I wanted to play baseball and then go to college, and it was a big disappointment to him that I didn't."

"How come you chose baseball?"

"Well I always loved baseball, and I saw one major league game and they didn't impress me that much, so I felt like I could become a big league ballplayer."

"Did your son play baseball?"

"Dick played some baseball when he was young, and unfortunately he played on a team that wasn't too good, they were always getting beat by big scores, and I didn't have much opportunity to see him play in those days because, y'know, most of the games at that time were in the late afternoon or early evenings and of course we had to be at the ball park two and a half hours before the game, so consequently I didn't have much time to spend with my son in sports."

"What position did he play?"

"He played the outfield. But after a while he got away from it, turned to football, and he played on a very good CBC team. They were undefeated coupla years, he was a halfback, started off as a guard, which is a tough position, but he had good speed. He and Mike Shannon, who's a Cardinal announcer now, they were on the same team together and they had some terrific years."

"Were you disappointed he didn't follow you?"

"No, I wasn't. Y'know, we let him do his own thing, with all our children, and Dick in particular. And he ran track at Notre Dame, and went out for football for about a week!" Musial laughed with that warm, engaging grin. "Yeah, Hank Stram had him come to Notre Dame, though he was smaller in stature than the Notre Dame guys, but he was a good football player and he was tough, ran the 220 on the Notre Dame track team."

"What's he do now?"

"Well he's been part of our operations in St. Louis, our restaurants and hotels, our bowling alleys. He's been running our hotels here in Florida for five–six years now, runnin' the Hilton Hotel in St. Louis at the airport, been in the business for fifteen–twenty years."

"What didn't you get in life by being a ballplayer? Any regrets?"

"No, that's the only thing I wanted to do was be a big league ballplayer, I loved baseball and I played it all the time. I used to play four–five–six hours every day, and although I played basketball, too, I just loved baseball better, it's a great game. I had a neighbor who loved baseball, too, and he managed a team in our plant that he was working in in those days, and I was their water boy for half a season. Then one day the pitcher didn't show up and he put me into the game and I did very well, and they voted me onto the team. Of course, I was only fifteen–sixteen in those days, which was good experience for me, because I was competing against guys who were twenty and twenty-one and I was doing very well as a pitcher for this team."

"You think you would've made it as a pitcher?"

"No, I doubt if I'd ever become a Warren Spahn. Y'know, when you're in high school and you have a good arm—and I could throw hard—they always make you the pitcher. Although when I wasn't pitching, I hit fourth and played the outfield, I was always a good hitter, even in high school. But they made me a pitcher and, of course, I was wild. And even when I pitched for a year or two in the minor leagues, I was awful wild. I walked six, eight guys a game and didn't have any confidence in pitching, whereas I had confidence in my hitting, I had good speed and I could catch the ball."

"When my oldest son first started playing baseball, he turned out to be a natural left-handed hitter and I modeled his stance somewhat on yours, coming out of a crouch, and ever since, all his coaches have been trying to change it."

"Well, of course, the most important thing is bein' comfortable at the plate and really not try to copy anybody. Anything that comes natural, that's the best way to do it. But y'know, Ben Hogan told me one time, 'You have the best stance in baseball.' And I said, 'Ben, why is that?' He said, ' 'Cause your bat is already back in a hitting position. That's the same swing you come out of a golf swing."

"Did you ever learn anything from Ted Williams about hitting?"

"No, we didn't have much time to talk about hitting, I'd see him down in spring training here, play the All-Star games together, but never had a chance to really talk baseball. I've seen him more in the last couple of years at the Hall of Fame ceremonies and we had some chance to talk, but we never talk about our hitting styles."

"Was he the best hitter you've ever seen?"

"Yes, indeed. He was very scientific, and he studied hitting, studied pitchers, and he was just outstanding."

"What would you've done had you not played baseball?"

"I probably've been a coach if I had gone to college, I liked athletics, loved sports, loved teaching, loved coaching and being around sports, so I'd've been in that capacity somewhere."

"Do you regret not having gone to college?"

"Well that's the only thing, I don't really have any regrets because I've had such an outstanding career in baseball and it opened so many doors for me in other lines and businesses. So I don't regret it, although I wish I would've had a college education, and probably after my baseball career, if I had gone to college, I probably would've gotten into politics."

"How would you like to be remembered as a father?"

"Well, y'know, now my children are all grown up, they have families of their own, they've all had college educations, though I'd give most of my credit to my wife, raisin' the kids and givin' them advice and bein' with them, so I'd say I'd just like to be remembered as a, y'know, good father."

As we headed down the ramp together toward the clubhouse in the now nearly empty ball park, I couldn't resist asking him to show me that famous stance once more. And I swear a shudder ran through me as Stan the Man stood before us "uncoiling like a spring," laughing, then shaking our hands, and immediately surrounded by fans asking for his autograph.

But I was still humming joyously inside. "Guys!" I burst out as we continued down the echoing ramp, "can you believe it, in one day meeting *Ted Williams* and *Stan Musial?*"

"All right, Dad, calm down, calm down," and my sons kept smiling beside me.

Into the Cardinal clubhouse we went to interview Ozzie Smith—without question, in our minds, supreme among fielding shortstops. For no one in my day—not Rizzuto, Carrasquel, nor Aparicio—had ever played the position with such grace and élan, those brilliant ballet moves and acrobatic jetés. The three of us dazzled last summer during an NBC *Game of the Week* when he flung his body flat-out through the air and parallel to the ground for a wicked one-hopper and, in a single seamless motion, speared it backhand in the hole, bounced instantly off the Astroturf, and came up firing to nail the runner on a bang-bang play. And Vin Scully adding it was the bounce that was most astounding. "How could he get back up so fast? His body must be made of rubber. Remarkable!"

And now there we were in a corner of the Cardinal clubhouse with the wondrous "Wizard of Oz," looking slighter than the five-ten he was listed at in the program as he pedaled away on the bicycle machine and softly talked.

"Did your father play sports?"

"No, my father wasn't very athletically oriented, I guess. People ask me where my athletic ability comes from and I think it came from my mother's side of the family."

"Yes, well in all the years I've watched you, in the best sense of the word, you seem to me softer: gentle, sensitive, and, therefore, I assume your mother's influence was a big part of your life?"

"Well it definitely was. I think with most black athletes anyway, they usually come from a broken home, and I'm no different in that aspect. My dad wasn't around, really, when I got seriously involved in baseball and I was pretty much reared by my mother."

"What were you praised for as a child?"

"For everything, doing the very best that I could do, caring, being sensitive toward other people."

"What kind of praise do you give O.J., your three-year-old son?"

"Everything, too. But I'm still conscious of never forcing him into doing what I do. You know, if he chooses to do that, then that's fine. But I'm not going to say, 'Hey, here's a baseball and here's a bat and this is what you've got to do.' I want him to choose what it is he does, and whatever it is he chooses to do, I'm gonna give him as much support as I possibly can. If he's proud of something and feels good about it, then I praise him for that."

"Twenty-eight years ago, when you were three years old in Watts, it was a different world. What were the differences for your son at three and you at three?"

"Well I didn't have all the things that he has now. We weren't rich, but we weren't poor, either. A lot of people play off the fact that hey, they grew up in bad neighborhoods and things like that, but that to me really has nothin' to do with where you end up. As long as you were able to get out and you survived, you took advantage of an opportunity, and that's more important to me."

"Were there many players growing up with you who never made it in sports but could have?"

"Well I think you can always find some guys you grew up with in that situation. The percentage of guys makin' it to the big leagues is one in every ten thousand or something, so once you make it here, you definitely have to feel that you're in an elite group."

"What would you have done if you hadn't been a ballplayer?"

"Hard to say. You know, I was one year away from my degree in social science at Cal Poly, so it might've been something with a teaching background. I think I would've been working with young kids somehow."

"Finally, Ozzie, how would you like to be remembered as a father?"

"I'd like to be remembered as a dad who was caring, sharing, giving, not too demanding, very supportive, and overall a good person."

Which is exactly the way I found him.

Leaving the clubhouse, we passed Red Schoendienst, who still moves with such fluidity through my memories —to this day I've never seen a second baseman glide as gracefully to a ball as he did—not that Tommy Herr's lead-footed, far from it. But what a peerless double-play combination Ozzie and Schoendienst would've made! Red was being interviewed, too, for Cardinal radio, and as he sat there listening to the reporter's questions, he looked somehow like a sad old sea turtle with his drooping mouthlines and baggy eyes. Why, I wondered, was he so sad? At being sixty-three? He must have money, still loves baseball? Then why so sad? Too long on the road? Away from his family? The game leaving little time for anything else?

I wasn't sure as yet.

\* \* \*

Next afternoon, we were off to Clearwater's Jack Russell Stadium to see Mike Schmidt and Richie Ashburn. And if I thought Al Lang Field was old-fashioned baseball, this was like déjà vu at the Phillies' bandbox park, like Ebbets Field in the late '40s or early '50s when I first began going to games, with its hometown hoardings on the outfield fences: Clearwater Plumbing, Havco Paints, Lenny's Restaurant, and a huge Marlboro Man in deep left center. (I would later come to find there was a Marlboro sign in every ball park we visited.)

Up to the small press box we went—the boys were getting blasé about this now, veteran observers—to see Richie Ashburn, the former brilliant center fielder who spent fifteen years in the majors with a lifetime average of .308, won two batting titles, and overall, caught more flyballs than any other outfielder in the history of the game. Now fifty-nine, he'd been a Phillies' broadcaster for the past twenty-four years, with his ever-present pipe and white hair, though he was still the fresh-faced, blond-haired Nebraska farmboy to me—and long overdue in the Hall of Fame.

His father had been a pretty good semipro second baseman back in Tilden, Nebraska, he told me, playing what was known as town team baseball.

"He was a pretty fair hitter and a good fielder, but, of course, not good enough to be a professional. He worked like most people, and usually on Saturdays and Sundays, they played ball. But he was my first, Oh, I guess you'd call him my first coach or manager. I was a catcher and he would pitch, and my brother would—I have a brother who's two years older—stand at the plate and deliberately miss it, so I'd get used to the swinging bat and the ball coming. And my father's the one who put the bat on my left shoulder. I was always a left-hand hitter."

"But you threw right?"

"Threw right, yes."

"Was he critical of you in any way?"

"Mostly he was supportive. If he got critical, he got critical when I got into the major leagues. He wanted me to go for more power. His expression was, 'Get down on the end of the bat and swing it like a man.' Well, I'm sure he meant well, but in my particular case, I think it was more important for me to make contact with the ball consistently and use my speed than try to hit an occasional long ball. I think I probably could've hit a few more home runs with that approach, but I think the other approach was far better for me."

"What's your relationship with your sons?"

"Well, my first son, Richard, had a tryout with the Phillies, and he was a good high school player. He pitched a no-hitter or two in high school, but he was also an outfielder, and he could've been a first baseman-third baseman. He had a tryout down here one spring, but he didn't make it. Now, this sounds like a father speaking about his son, but I feel had they stayed with him—he was a late bloomer, I saw him play and I tried to be objective about seeing my son play, he was a switch-hitter and he had a lot of power, bigger and stronger, he was 'bout six foot three, 190-pounder, and I saw him hit balls from both sides of the plate that I mean I just could've never done myself—and I felt had they stuck with him, he may've developed."

"What was his reaction?"

"I think he was disappointed, but, you know, he went on with his life, and he's doing very well as a manufacturer's representative in the Philadelphia area. And my other son, John, might've been a better football player. They were both big kids. As so often happens, Richard didn't really have the drive for it, and John did, but he didn't have Richard's ability. Had somehow they been able to get that mix together, I think one of them might've made professional baseball."

"Do you see any similarities to the way you parented your sons and the way your father did?"

"Very little, very little. The difference was my dad used to take a willow switch to me once in a while when I was a kid, and probably I deserved it, but I never did that with my boys. I know my dad was stricter with me in terms of schoolwork and that kind of thing—he wasn't strict with me in sports 'cause he didn't have to be, I loved sports, I couldn't wait to get into baseball, basketball, football, track, any of it. And I never really had that problem with my sons, either, though I didn't get to see them play as much as I would like. But I don't think my sons were subjected to that much good baseball coaching and managing. 'Cause I saw it, I heard what coaches and managers *said* to them, and I think they said a lot of the wrong things. Now, I did not interfere with that. Maybe I should've, I don't know."

"Willie Mays, in his autobiography, says that more youngsters who might've had a future in baseball are turned off by overcoaching in their teens."

"Well, in my own case, I saw some very *bad* coaching. I mean, let's face it, most of these kids are not going to be professional baseball players, but, on the other hand, some of them might've had a chance with the proper instruction."

"What did you give up by playing ball? Any regrets?"

"Well, I always wanted to be a lawyer, believe it or not. It's funny, the lawyer I have in Philadelphia always wanted to be a baseball player, and he's been down to these Baseball Dream Weeks they have. Well, if they ever had a Lawyers' Dream Week, I think I'd go to that. The only regret I might have is baseball was so important to me, it was so number one that number two was a long way back. And you know, I had a wife and kids, and I think now that it's all over that they sacrificed a lot for me and because of me, and maybe I shouldn't have put baseball in such a high priority. But, on the other hand, maybe I wouldn't have done as well had I *not* put it there. So that's all speculation and I'm just guessing about that."

"Has your wife ever commented about it?"

"No, no, she was a very good baseball wife—you

know, they practically raise the kids—and we had six kids, it was a chore. But I have a daughter who is a writer and she has written a couple of things that really made me think. I remember one thing, in a column she wrote one time, that when they were growing up, they hoped that I wouldn't make the All-Star team so I'd have those three days off at home with the family. And that really got to me. It put things in a better perspective."

"What about when your baseball career was over? Did you go right into broadcasting?"

"I went right into it, although I didn't think I would. At that time, I had some political aspirations, I was the Young Republican chairman in the state of Nebraska for a few years, and I did a lot of work for Eisenhower and Nixon in the Midwest, and later on, Barry Goldwater, and I had some aspirations to run for Congress out there. Then I was offered this broadcasting job and turned it down, and it was in the wintertime after I'd retired, and they said, 'Well, think about it a month or two, we have plenty of time.' So I did, and my wife was opposed to the political arena, so I took the broadcasting job."

"Any regrets when your baseball career ended?"

"My only regret was I had a chance at 3,000 hits had I kept playing, and I wound up with a few short of 2,600. But I ended my career with such a terrible team, the Mets, we lost 120 games. And when you're late in your career with a bad team, that doesn't give you much motivation or much to look forward to."

"How would you like to be remembered as a father?"

"Well, a loving father, certainly number one. And a caring father. And I think I am that. I feel very strongly that I am, and I think my relationship with my children is, I'd say, maybe better than it's ever been. They're older now, they're probably a little more understanding."

"When I was twelve years old, I had a friend, a fanatical baseball fan like myself, who went to a Giant game at the Polo Grounds to see you play and he sat behind the dugout. His image of ballplayers in those days was that they didn't smoke, drink, use obscenity, and you were his hero. And I saw him the next day and he said he couldn't believe it, 'Ashburn cursed a blue streak from the beginning of the game to the end.'"

"I could do that, yeah, though I doubt if I cursed from beginning to end. See, my family has never heard me curse, I don't think anybody out of the dugouts has ever heard me curse, I never cursed off the field. But on the field—I know my wife, who was sitting down by the dugout one time, heard me and I mean she couldn't believe it. She was shocked at the stuff that was comin' out of this mild-mannered guy that she was supposedly living with. But, you know, I got mad. I hated pitchers on the other team, I hated some of the players, some of the managers—and if it was the Polo Grounds, I'm guessing Leo Durocher was the manager, some of the things we used to call him, you'd get locked up for today!"

After the Orioles made the final out of their exhibition game, we hustled down to the Phillies' clubhouse, the boys a bit nervous upon entering but trying to appear cool, like part of the scene, waiting for Mike Schmidt to get dressed, stocky Steve Jeltz and whooping crane Kent Tekulve passing by with "Hi's", Geordie casually "Hi"-ing back, Ceo shyly nodding, and Schmidt apparently ready, motioning us over in the now all but deserted locker room. And seated side by side on two wooden stools, Mike, with his Paul Newman blue eyes, slightly pitted cheeks, and thoughtful, granite air, took a long time between answers:

"My father was a really good athlete in high school in Dayton, Ohio, and then he got drafted into World War II, and, of course, that stopped any chance of him ever doing anything. But he never played any professional sports, no."

"Did he encourage you?"

"Yeah, all the time. In fact, I think I owe where I am now, I owe a great deal of that to my dad and his willingness to stand behind me and make sure I always had baseballs and footballs and equipment to play with and a place to play. He was a contributor and a sponsor of organized Little Leagues, sponsored a senior Little League team, and was involved considerably in all organized baseball when I was a kid."

"Did that bring you closer together?"

"Oh, absolutely. I came from a very, very loving, family-oriented environment, and I think that means a great deal to a guy."

"Was he critical in any way of you?"

"Everything I did. Everything I did. I was really never good enough for him. He was on me all the time, and I think he was proud of me and what I accomplished as a young kid, but I think he always wanted to make it clear to me that I could always be better than I was. So he never was one that walked around and bragged about his son. He was a very quiet man—or *is* a very quiet man, still is. He can still sit in Riverfront Stadium in Cincinnati and not bat an eye if I hit a couple of home runs in a game. He's very unemotional—and I'm a lot like him."

"Were you fulfilling a dream of his by becoming a ballplayer?"

"Well, I don't think my father ever was close enough to organized baseball to ever feel like he came up short or anything like that. You know, I feel like whatever I would've ended up doing, my father would've been behind me. But no, I don't think I'm fulfilling a dream of his."

"Would you like your son to be a ballplayer?"

"Well, at this point I just want him to do what he wants to do, what he feels comfortable doing. If it's a professional athlete, a lawyer, a piano player, a plumber, whatever, so long as he strives for excellence, as long as he puts his all into whatever he attempts to do, I'll be proud of him or I'll be behind him a 100 percent."

"I know as a single parent of these two teenage boys, I sometimes hear my father's voice in mine. Does that happen to you?"

"Oh, all the time, all the time. I even use some of his old sayings from time to time with my five-year-old son. The way my father handled me, as I look back on it, was outstanding. I wouldn't want it any other way."

"You don't feel you're overcritical with your son?"

"Well, he's still too young for him to be competing or to be really doing anything where it's time for me to really keep an eye on how he goes about things. He's still a baby."

"Any regrets about becoming a ballplayer?"

"Not really. Though I've been playin' ball for twenty years, so I really don't know what it's like to live a normal summer. We had a strike one year and I got a little bit of a feel for what being a normal person is like."

"You don't think you've paid a price, then?"

"Paid a price? Yeah, I've been paying a price my whole life. Paying a price is hard to define. I don't know what you mean by that. I've worked hard to get where I am. I have sacrificed a lot of things in life to get where I am. I've put in a lot of sweat, a lot of workin' out, a lot of rehabilitation, came through a lot of injuries, put up with a lot of booing, learned to handle failure, I learned to handle being away from my family. You gotta give your family some credit, too, for stickin' with you and learnin' to live your kind of a routine. A lot of times a baseball life is not all that tough—I mean, guys'll say, 'Geez, I'd give anything to live a normal life.' Well, you know, I make two million dollars a year to be home a week and away a week and home a week and away a week, and go to the health club every morning in the off-season and have calluses on my hands, and when I go out the door here, I gotta sign fifty autographs and fight my way to my car. All the things you're talkin' about are 'paying the price,' so to speak, but they're all part of my life and they're all part of being where I'm at in playing the game at the level at which I've played it. And I guess if you asked me if I wanted to trade places with anybody, I would say no. There isn't a life on this earth that I'd rather have other than my own."

"What would you have done if you hadn't played ball?"

"I probably would've found a way to succeed in something. It depends on what you mean by succeed, or what I mean by succeed, but I would've found a way to find happiness in life, contentment. You know it might've been runnin' my dad's business, which means I would've been a soda jerk, I'd've dipped ice cream cones, I'd've been a—who knows what I would've done? I'd've been in the swimming pool business, I would've been somewhere, but I feel like I would've found a way to be content and happy in life."

"When you say successful, would it have to have been financially successful?"

"Absolutely not. See, I'm saying that now from hindsight. I'm saying that as a guy who's been rewarded financially extremely well, and it's easy for a guy like me to say, 'Hey, I would've been happy without any money or I would've been happy if I hadn't been able to buy that nice car, or, you know, if I would've had to watch every penny I spent, I wouldn't've been able to take those nice vacations, live in that big house.' It's easy for me to say I'd be happy without it, but I think right now if it were all taken away from me, I'd be fine."

"What do you see yourself doing when you retire?"

"I don't see myself really doing anything other than what the Lord has planned for me. And I don't know what that'll be."

"Have you laid out some goals?"

"Well, no, I really don't have any goals. I don't think my future is in my own hands, I think I'm gonna live life day to day and go at life the way I feel the good Lord would want me to go after it. And I feel like He'll put me in the spot that he wants me to best serve him in."

"Finally, how would you like to be remembered as a father?"

"Well I'd like to be known as a father that taught my son how to love, number one, in a really loving and caring and unselfish environment. Obviously I've been fortunate enough to be able to provide for my son, financially he'll be able to go to school, he'll be able to have nice things. I would like him to be able to someday sit down and say that 'My father taught me to appreciate nice things and that I'm very fortunate to have had a father who worked hard and was able to provide for me.' Maybe if my son says, 'I want to grow up and be like my dad,' that would be enough for me."

# Chapter Four

**J**ust before going through infield and outfield drill with Geordie and the JV, I spot Ceo down on the varsity diamond and walk across to meet him, thinking as I do of how long I've watched my sons. How many games and practices, from T-ball to high school now and all those warm-ups in between: Ceo's natural left-hand swing as a boy, his first grand slam, a towering shot to straightaway center off a Pony pitcher he'd always had trouble hitting, and Geordie, following in his footsteps, repeating the feat a year later in Bronco All-Stars. As an only child I'd played so many games alone, stickball, stoopball, dice baseball (which eventually became Strat-O-Matic), that this sharing with my sons has been like a second childhood for me, and I wouldn't trade a moment of it for the world.

# Chapter Five

**G**eorge Kell, the former Tiger third baseman and Hall of Famer, was down on the field with Al Kaline when we arrived at Lakeland that evening, so once more up to the press box we went to watch the tail end of Pittsburgh's batting practice. Jason Thompson and Steve Kemp were bombing long drives off the right-field light towers, à la Roy Hobbs. "Humungous!" exclaimed Ceo, gazing down on Marchant Stadium's green playing field aglow with an eerie phosphorescence under a dusky Florida sky as 4,200 fans filed in, and a couple of reporters behind us kept recalling all the Detroit announcers. Van Patrick, Harry Heilmann, and Ty Tyson, and someone came by with regards from Muskegon.

Which made me realize yet again just how regional and small-town baseball is. Coming from New York and now living in L.A., I usually think of the game as media-blitzed, metropolitan show biz and tend to forget its grass roots appeal: the semipro and minor league teams barnstorming through those bandbox ball parks, playing the one-horse towns, like touring companies of *The Music Man*; or that the Red Sox represent not only Massachusetts but also Vermont, New Hampshire, Rhode Island, a good part of Connecticut, and faraway Maine;

while the Tigers, Cubs, and Cardinals reach across the vast Midwest on the voices of Harry Caray, Jack Buck, Ty Tyson—and Ernie Harwell, suddenly beside me, who's been doing this for forty-seven years—as George Kell came bustling in, wearing a dark blue Tiger cap with my favorite Old English "D," now sixty-three but still looking vigorous and trim. He'd been another one of my heroes when I was a boy on Long Island and hated the pinstriped Yankees, and the Tigers had Dick Wakefield and Prince Hal Newhouser and would get close but never overtake those smug Bronx Bombers, who always managed to win: Tommy Henrich forever homering in the bottom of the ninth or Joe Page jumping the bullpen fence, warm-up jacket slung over his shoulder like a toreador, as he struck out the side once more with the bases loaded.

Standing in the doorway of the TV booth, the boys and I now listened to Kell's soothing Arkansas drawl tell us about his father, who'd been an outstanding amateur player.

"Probably one of the best of his time, and I followed him around, that's all we ever did was just play baseball. I said at my speech at Cooperstown, my father raised three sons and he was convinced they'd all be big league ballplayers. And two of us *did* play in the major leagues, one with the Philadelphia A's, and one got killed in the service. But my father knew it took a lot of growin' up to play the game, knew the problems, and he was very understanding."

"Did your son play?"

"No, he didn't. My son played American Legion ball, and finally just quit. He said it was too tough—you know, everybody said, 'Well, he don't play as good as his dad or he don't do this like his dad,' and he said it wasn't worth it."

Kell himself attended Arkansas State College for one year, in 1939. "And I promised my dad I'd go back if he'd let me sign a professional contract—and I still intend to go back," he added, laughing, "I haven't done it yet—No, I'm not going back! I just keep tellin' *him* that."

"What would you have done if you hadn't played ball?"

"Well that's a good question. I don't know. My wife was a schoolteacher, and I thought at one time about bein' a teacher and a coach, if I didn't make it, maybe in high school or college, and I think I would've got my degree."

"Was it a tough adjustment when it was over?"

"No, it wasn't for me, I went right into broadcasting. I went in the year I got out of baseball, that was twenty-eight years ago, and I been broadcasting for Detroit ever since, so I really didn't have an adjustment like a lotta guys. I didn't lay out a year or two years, I've stayed right with it. And I have my son with me now in an automobile agency in Newport, Arkansas. My son's forty years old, he's running the agency, and we're closer—we're like I had hoped we'd be twenty years ago."

"By the way, I'm sure you remember a game my

father and I saw nearly forty years ago when DiMaggio, with the bases loaded, hit a ground-ball shot that broke your jaw and you still made the play at third?"

"I could not forget it, could never forget it. He hit me right in the jaw, and I was gonna make a double play, and I wound up, I did get the guy at third base, I stepped on the bag, then collapsed and they took me to the hospital, wired my jaw, and I didn't play any more the rest of the year."

And shortly thereafter, like a religious ritual—as Kell took his seat behind the mike—fielding drills were completed, groundskeepers manicured the diamond, our national anthem struck up, four thousand strong standing and applauding as the chorus ended once more with "the home of the brave." And it was play ball in Lakeland! The geriatric ushers—"Old Foggos," Geordie called them with a smiling shake of his head—were escorting other geriatrics to their seats—one of whom, at eighty-five, claimed to have seen Ty Cobb, "the meanest son-of-a-bitch who ever wore a uniform—meaner even than Pete Rose." And the best Tiger he'd ever seen? "Oh, a tie, I'd have to say, between Charlie Gehringer and Al Kaline."

On the drive down to Clearwater, as we passed beside the dark orange groves, Geordie looked over at me and said, "Dad, you know, when I get older, I'm going to write the same book, take *my* kids to see all *my* heroes."

\* \* \*

The following day, under a flawless blue sky, we drove into the Dodgers' 450-acre complex at Vero Beach and were immediately thrust into another world. No longer the laid-back Red Sox facility nor the Phillies' bandbox ball park, we were now surrounded by TV and newspaper reporters in a friendly, busy, corporate atmosphere—though Holman Stadium, strangely enough, looked slightly shoddy, no fences but rather grassy banks rimming the outfield. Still, Tommy Lasorda—on the surface, at least—was warm and jovial, joking with my sons; and the players, from Guerrero (a week before he tore up his knee) to Reuss and Madlock, with his passel of kids, all seemed loose and easygoing as we headed toward the press room and a meeting with Vin Scully.

A recent Hall of Famer and the voice of the Dodgers for over thirty-five years, he'd begun in Brooklyn with Red Barber and Connie Desmond and now accompanied me nightly on the L.A. freeways with the briny accuracy of his play-by-play: "A high drive into deep left field, back goes Baker, a way back, to the track, to the wall—it's gone!"

He talked about his days as a Fordham center fielder and of the "remarkable" Willie Mays: "He probably could've played every position and been an All-Star at every one. We had three center fielders in New York then and they all had great power, they all had consummate grace and skill, but of the three, no one could field a ground-ball base hit like Mays. I mean, Mays fielded it like he was a shortstop. Snider had a built-in fear that the ball would go through his legs. But Mays was remarkable, just remarkable."

"Who was the best pitcher you ever saw?"

"Well, of course, there were so many, but the only pitcher I ever saw, who, after one inning, I would think might be pitching a no-hitter was Sandy Koufax. He'd get the side out in order, and you'd think, Uh-oh, he's liable to do it again tonight."

We emerged from the press room, blinking into hazy sunlight—and there was Sandy Koufax before us, looking somehow uncomfortable now in a blue Dodger warm-up jacket, watching Orel Hershiser throw. My father and I had gone to the opening game of the '63 World Series when he'd struck out the first five Yankees in a row, the fastest pitcher I'd ever seen. And here he was this morning politely greeting my sons.

Smaller than I imagined, gracious and refined with his grainy salt-and-pepper hair, thin neck, and probing eyes, Koufax had never been one of the guys, easy in the rough-and-tumble comaraderie of athletes, but rather reminded me of a science whiz or valedictorian spending some spare time with sports. Or was that just my limited image, that any ballplayer who even held a book in his hands was surely an intellectual? For by his own admission, he'd had no interest as a boy in anything *except* sports, was an indifferent student, never had any overwhelming ambitions, and, most of all, was a loner who still kept his private life obsessively to himself—the J. D. Salinger of baseball.

When I asked him about his children, I was surprised to discover he didn't have any (though I knew he'd been married to Richard Widmark's daughter), and he didn't want to talk about his father (I later learned his real father had left when he was three, and he'd been raised by a stepfather, whose surname he'd adopted).

But he was more than happy to talk baseball. And for the next ten minutes or so, he was kind enough to give Geordie some pitching instruction as Ceo and I watched in wonder. Like Williams, he was gentle but insistent, observing Geordie's motion without a ball, then following with advice, "Don't lean too far back in your windup; that makes it tougher to keep the ball low. Keep your windup as compact as you can; a smaller windup will help your control. And don't count on your arm, don't overthrow; throw with your legs. If you get ahead of the hitter and make good pitches, you're going to make him hit *your* pitch, and that's what good pitching is all about."

Afterward, on our way to the Dodgers-Twins game, Geordie confessed he'd been so nervous, his legs were literally shaking when he threw.

And Orel Hershiser joined us as we walked along. Thin and gangly, with his horsy teeth and boyish grin, he was coming off a fantastic 19-3, 2.03 ERA season—though I could just as easily see him carting milk pails or bringing in the cows with his two-year-old son, Orel V. His father had played mostly hockey and "not a whole lot of baseball" in Buffalo, where he was raised.

"But I always tried to impress him. He was my number one fan and the number one guy I wanted to be excited about me doing well. I didn't really care about other fathers or even brothers and sisters, but if my dad thought I had a good game, that was important to me."

"Did it bring you closer together?"

"Yeah, it did. Especially when I did well. But when I did poorly, sometimes I felt distance from him because I felt like I'd disappointed him. And now, being older, I know I wasn't disappointing him, he was just there to help. But he was a traveling salesman, and when he would come off a plane and right to the Little League field, I didn't want him to be let down that I'd had a bad game."

From Vero we drove south the next morning to Fort Lauderdale and our final stop with the Yankees—and ran head-on into the ultimate big business franchise and home of the *macho* corporate swagger. The boys were denied access to the clubhouse due to the new league rules, designed apparently to inhibit drug trafficking, excluding anyone without an authorized pass. So they had to wait in the car as I alone watched Dave Winfield strut and pose, and curtly refuse to be interviewed, or Whitey Ford squirt his stream of tobacco juice as he squeezed his beery paunch into a uniform—both he and

Mantle would respond to me, I'd been informed earlier, only if they were paid. Both felt they'd been ripped off during their playing days and now had it coming to them. And this, the baseball of today: TV ratings, lucrative commercials, and, for the first time ever, a way to be a millionaire as opposed to being a great (albeit underpaid) athlete, or as Mantle himself had said, "It's now like twenty-five separate corporations coming to the ball park." Williams, for example, received a ten-thousand-dollar raise after hitting .406 in 1941. And not that other stars from smaller major league cities were that different (Pete Rose had charged Geordie seven dollars for his autograph at a baseball card show in L.A. last fall), but without the big-city limelight and media blitz, it seemed easier to get on with the fun of playing this kid's game for what it was and, at its basic level, would somehow always be.

To be sure, there were other Yankees, like Don Mattingly, who appeared essentially shy, self-contained, and out of place, never once parading about like a peacock his immense talents on the field—and happy to talk, but not now, he was besieged, and I'd have to wait till the summer, when we got to New York.

So I soon left, walking out alone, nobody around in the fading Florida twilight as I turned the corner—and found myself face to face with Joe DiMaggio in a natty blue blazer and gray flannel slacks. White-haired and courtly with a still-powerful grip, he was so controlled, he seemed to be locked in a display case, the price he'd had to pay for that peerless grace under pressure. He'd been a pitchman for Mr. Coffee to my sons' generation, but to me he'd always be The Yankee Clipper, serenely patrolling the Stadium's great green meadow of center field or, more impressively, unleashing that smooth, titanic swing. I can still vividly recall a straight line drive never rising at all as it went soaring over Gil Coan's head toward the monuments in dead center for a triple.

The greatest player Williams had ever seen, DiMaggio, now seventy-one, talked about growing up in Martinez, California, and playing basketball as a kid with Hank Luisetti.

"There was no grass and we played baseball on asphalt, too, with a big ball—a softball—but we threw it overhand and played regular baseball rules. Later on, when I was eleven or twelve, I started playing with older fellas, guys in their twenties. I guess they saw something in me."

"And at seventeen you were playing Triple-A shortstop with the San Francisco Seals."

"Yes, well my arm was very, very strong—strong enough to break the seats back of first base—but not at all accurate. My father, who was a California fisherman, thought the game was football and was afraid that I'd be hurt."

"Did he encourage you when you were growing up?"

"No, as a matter of fact. You have to start with Vince, who was the first to enter professional baseball, and Dad was not too pleased with that. He didn't know that you could earn a living at it, and he thought it was something that shiftless people got into. Then when Vince broke in with Tucson in the Arizona League and then with San Francisco, of course that changed his mind, and when I broke in, it changed it even more."

I'd heard many stories about his son, Joe, Jr., apparently small and plump and very quiet, some authenticated, others not: that he'd gone to the prestigious Lawrenceville prep school, been a Marine, was never an athlete, had a nervous breakdown, and that his father had gotten him a job in northern California at a savings and loan, then bought him a truck, but he'd received so many tickets, he'd lost that, too, and was now so estranged that the only time anyone ever heard from him was when he was in trouble or needed money.

And Joe, of course, wouldn't discuss him, as he had to go. We exchanged another firm handshake and he continued on toward the Yankee clubhouse.

It was still early—six-thirty or so—when the Orioles arrived, pulling up without fanfare in their nondescript team bus, few reporters in sight, and were ushered into a tiny, cramped, and altogether drab dressing room. And a short time later I conducted my final spring-training interviews with probably the most famous father-son combination in baseball, Cal Ripken, Sr., and his son Cal, Jr.

Cal, Sr., was fifty (my age in three months), but somehow seemed older with his gaunt features, intense blue eyes, and lonesome cowboy look. He had never made the majors, playing seven years in the minors, and his son had become the star, winning Rookie of the Year in '82 and MVP in '83. Yet the father had become a fixture in his own right as the Orioles' third-base coach, after managing fourteen years in the minors in such far-flung towns as Leesburg, Florida; Appleton, Wisconsin; Aberdeen, South Dakota; Pasco, Washington; and Elmira, New York (and finally becoming Baltimore's skipper for that long and disappointing '87 season).

We sat on metal chairs some distance behind the batting cage as he stubbed out one Lucky Strike after another and glanced down before answering.

"What's the one memory you have of your son as a boy?"

"I guess probably the biggest memory with him is the fact of his desire to wanna play baseball, and every time you turned around, he hadda ball and a glove. He was ready to play at any time."

"My sons play ball, too, and I know the feeling of suddenly 'being them.' Do you ever have that feeling with him?"

"No, not at all. Because in this business—and I've been in it for thirty years—I had a lotta young guys, and when he was coming along in pro ball, he was another young guy coming along. Fortunately, he was a young guy coming along with a lot of ability and I could recognize that ability, but I never lived through him, in any way."

"Did your father play sports?"

"No, my father didn't play, but I had two brothers, one brother played pro ball and the other brother would've played pro ball, but there was always sports in the family."

"Did your dad encourage you to play as a boy?"

"Well, unfortunately, my father was killed when I was nine years old, so it was more my mom. I don't think there was any encouragement to play, and I don't think I encouraged Cal or Billy, who's a minor league infielder, or any of our kids to play. I was always a firm believer that you go do what you wanna do. If you wanna play, then that's fine, go ahead and do it and have fun at it and enjoy it. If you wanna continue to do that and you wanna make your livelihood out of it, then the thing to do is go out, give it the best you can—and if they had a question, my door was always open. But really, I wasn't around that much when Cal was growing up and playing ball in particular, because I was away managing and he was home in school."

"If you hadn't played ball, what would you have done?"

"I have no idea what I would've done. I loved soccer, and, of course, if soccer would've been as prevalent years ago with the money being available as it is today with the North American Soccer League, I may've played soccer. But I don't know, there's so many things that I enjoy doin'. I like electrical work, I like carpentry, I oughta been a groundskeeper. There isn't anything that I've found that I've done that I haven't enjoyed doin'," and he stubbed out his Lucky Strike.

At six-four, Cal, Jr., was five inches taller than his father, muscular and good-looking, with a free and easy charm as he talked about his upbringing.

"My dad never forced us to do anything, he always seemed to go along with whatever we wanted to do. It wasn't as if he took us out and said, 'Okay, you're gonna play baseball, that's what you're gonna do.' It was nothing like that. When we played basketball or soccer, we seemed to always have a soccer ball or a place to play, or if he had time, he would show us how. But he just kinda let us go our own way and develop our own interests."

"Was he critical of you in any way?"

"Not really, no, not too much. Only if my behavior in a certain sport embarrassed me or I might've acted like a fool on the field, y'know, threw a temper tantrum or I threw my helmet or was arguin' with the umpires. If you did somethin' that he thought was outta line, then he would say somethin'. But I mean he never was over-critical about your play. If you messed up a game or lost, he would never come up and say, 'Hey, y'know you blew that game, you should practice harder, and do this and that.' He was very sympathetic."

"Did baseball bring you closer together?"

"Well it's an odd story. My dad was always there in the summertime when I wanted him, because I worked out with him in an atmosphere such as this. We were at a minor league ball park, he ran the show, and I would be hangin' around, pickin' up things on my own. But when I began playin' organized baseball, he never had the time. It was always my mom was the one who was there, takin' me to the game, consoling me afterwards if I gave up a home run in the last inning or tellin' me I did a great job if I pitched a no-hitter and drove in a couple runs. It was always my mom that was there."

"What do you think you've missed by becoming a ballplayer?"

"Well it was always in my mind to be a professional ever since I was eleven–twelve years old, hangin' around ball parks like this. I came outta high school and went straight into the Appalachian League in Bluefield, West Virginia. Most of my friends, of course, went the college route and they came back with stories that 'College is so much fun, it's a continuation of high school, you'd've really liked this and you'd've really liked that,' so I did feel like I was missing something in that respect. But actually I always kept in perspective that this is what I wanna do, it's the right thing for me, and those guys are missing what *I'm* doing. So I mean I kinda tried to turn things around so they'd be in my favor."

"Finally, what's the one memory you have as a child about your father?"

"Well the thing I most remember was the time that we spent at minor league parks, he always tappin' me on the leg and sayin', 'You wanna go with Dad today and shag flyballs?' Because I was too small actually to be in the infield and too small to hit, so we'd put the uniform on and I'd go in the outfield and shag the balls, and throw 'em back in. I'll always remember that, him tappin' me on the leg and sayin', 'You wanna go with me today?' Seemed like the highlight of my day. I waited for that."

We shook hands and he jogged out to shortstop as I headed back to my sons waiting in the car, and passing below the left-field stands, a young boy leaned down and asked, "Can I shake your hand?" I glanced around to see which of the players he wanted, but he was talking to me, and I said sure. Who was I? Someone on the field? Who'd just talked to the Ripkens? But I might also be some star of the past or TV sportscaster. Whatever, I had for one brief moment crossed that magic line that separates the game and the spectator, the dream and the reality, the player and the fan—and in many cases, fathers and sons, who ofttimes were fulfilling their father's dreams.

Sunday we flew back to L.A. with Geordie still holding his "rad" ball in his hand and once more chattering away, Ceo telling him to stop acting like a "Lame-o!" and musing himself about Williams, and me smiling and gazing out the window at the landscape below, thinking what a priceless legacy this had been for them already and that in July we'd begin anew, across the country and the rest of the interviews with baseball fathers and baseball sons, starting in L.A. with Rod Carew.

# Chapter Six

**B**ut meanwhile, back in Calabasas, my own son is coming to bat. One out, no score, bottom of the first, and I'm down in the third-base-coach's box, flashing him the bunt sign, clapping my hands together and chanting, "Come on, Geordie, start it off, start it off, good stroke up there, good stroke!" But he pops the first pitch foul, then calls time out to confer with me.

"Dad, I can hit this guy, lemme hit away, I don't wanna bunt."

"Okay, go 'head."

And on the next pitch, he smacks a wicked line drive, but right into the third baseman's glove. And I think again of my friend's comment, "It's enough your being their father without having to be their coach, too." But also of that incident with Ceo shortly before we left for Chicago last July.

The three of us had been growing increasingly impatient to get going, school for them was over, and I'd just passed gasping and still unbelieving into my fiftieth year. A few weeks after my birthday, we were all intently watching the climactic wrestling scene in the film *Vision Quest* on TV, when suddenly Ceo bounced straight up off his couch and challenged me to a match: "I can beat you,

Dad!" I smiled, shaking my head, but he kept persisting, "Come on, Dad, you know you can't win." And Geordie, seemingly upset at the prospect, intervening with, "Ceo, no, he doesn't want to do it, let's just watch the movie." But Ceo was unrelenting, "Come on, Dad!" jazzed up by the scenes on the screen and accompanying driving sound track of Tangerine Dream and Madonna, "I can beat you in basketball one-on-one (which he'd recently done) and I can beat you now in wrestling!" Geordie still trying to intercede—till I finally, reluctantly agreed.

And we began, with Ceo insisting I start on top, quickly astonished at how strong he'd become at sixteen, twisting and skidding over the living-room carpet, locked in each other's arms, no pins, getting him in a chokehold and having to break it—since it's illegal—then a full nelson —and having to break that, too, but realizing if we'd gone to a decision, his strength and speed would've surely worn me down.

Ceo was proud as could be, claiming he'd won— Geordie calling it a draw—and next day there were burn marks on my elbows as I told him, he still beaming, "You know, you really got strong."

Though, later that night, I couldn't stop replaying a recurring scene of my father and me wrestling at exactly the same ages, of how painful it'd been, and not wanting to get into that daily routine with my son, loving him far too much. My father's 220 pounds holding down my furious struggles for the opening minutes till, as he weakened, I was able to flip him over and bend his futile arm aching with bursitis into a hammerlock and make him give. Day after day I won and never felt any delight, if I expected delight, in the victory—for one never really succeeds over one's father, forty pounds lighter or not. The word "Dad" somewhere catching in my throat, and always a wince when said.

My father, a slope-shouldered Ralph Bellamy with his distinguished graying temples, raccoon eyes, double chin, and that Coca-Cola smile always primed for customers, friends, and family alike, trying to ignore our "differences" with truism after truism—and once finding, on a supposed clean-up campaign as he leafed through my papers, probed through my desk, some notes for a story that told of a dream. "Writing's OK, but you've still gotta earn a living. When I was your age, I had the same thoughts. The same ideas. But you'll see, you'll change. Everyone goes through stages like that. You'll look back later and see how silly your ideas were."

And looking back now, after years of rationalizing, patronizing, correcting his slightest grammatical error, what I recall is all those wrestling matches, the haunting fact of two children lost in infancy, and overly healthy me with 20/10 vision and never a broken bone, his "Tarzan," lone joy and creation, and the criticism of his eyes when I didn't reach perfection, that list of expected achievements: going to Harvard instead of Cornell; a four-letter athlete; marrying a beautiful, extremely wealthy Jewish girl; coming into and eventually taking over his business; settling down safe and secure in the suburbs, joining the Shriners, the Masons, the UJA, well-thought-of and religious in the community, and bringing up a brood of well-liked, good-natured children who at birth are enrolled at Harvard and, at age three, stroll about the ranch-house lawn clad in crimson T-shirts—I drifted increasingly away from his dreams. At age ten, he would tell me stories and dandle me upon his knee, or, on those bright, windy Saturdays a few years later, we would watch Ted Williams at the Stadium together. This shy man who won a swimming medal in his youth and was a social director in the Catskills in his twenties, worked with his father in their restaurant, Wimmer's of Fordham Road, and together saw Ruth and Cobb and even Honus Wagner play. He once confided to me, his eyes navigating the carpet, that at nineteen he broke his virginity and went uptown to a whore, dragged by a bumptious uncle of mine, then, married at thirty, avoided intercourse during the courtship because it wasn't the right thing to do. He would rant at my parading nudity if I came out of the shower without a towel, "Put something on! Cover up your business!" or hastily shut the bathroom door whenever I found him shaving in just an old-fashioned undershirt—and who always thought he would retire at fifty, then fifty-five in his seven-in-the-morning-to-seven-at-night-and-most-Saturdays dedication to the business—before abruptly dying, eight months after finally retiring, of a stroke at sixty-nine.

# Chapter Seven

Rod Carew was born on a train in Panama, had rheumatic fever as a child, and his father, a local house painter, never thought he was tough enough. As he says in his book on hitting, "I was in and out of the hospital a lot, something that irritated him because he believed little boys should be tough (like my brother), so I was physically abused at times. I mean, there wasn't a time in my life I wasn't kicked, or punched, or whipped, often for no reason whatsoever." When he was fourteen, his mother left his father, and, with his three sisters, Rod immigrated to New York City.

He attended George Washington High School in the Bronx, but spent so much time learning English that he wasn't able to try out for the baseball team—and anyway, the coach had already told him he wasn't good enough to make the club. So he played sandlot ball instead and signed with the Twins when he graduated. Through nineteen seasons in the majors, he compiled a .328 lifetime average with 3,053 hits, and won the batting title seven times. In 1970, he married Marilynn Levy, a white, middle-class, Jewish girl, and they have three daughters, ages thirteen, ten, and eight.

The boys and I met him at a nearby bookshop where

he was signing copies of *Rod Carew's Art and Science of Hitting,* and there I found an elegant, soft-spoken man with finely chisled bones and a quiet, though fiercely controlled intensity.

"Have you encouraged your children to play sports?"

"Well, I've encouraged them to participate and have fun, because I think that at a young age that's what youngsters are supposed to do. It gives them a chance to meet other youngsters and learn about kids with different backgrounds and make friends, and that's what I've tried to stress more."

"Were you encouraged to play when you were young?"

"I was encouraged by my mother and an uncle who raised me. My dad didn't take the time to work with me and encourage me to play, he was more critical—I guess I wasn't his favorite son—so I was fortunate to have two other people who really did."

"What was he critical of?"

"I guess of everything I did. I was a very sick kid growing up, and he didn't feel that I could do anything, so I got myself into baseball and I kept saying that I'm gonna work at it until maybe one day I'm gonna be good."

"Do you ever hear his voice in yours with your children?"

"No, I don't, because I know what I went through and they're not gonna go through that."

"Are you critical of your children?"

"Well, one thing I try to do is *not* be critical of them when they play. I want them to enjoy this stage of their life as youngsters, so I stop what I'm doing to help them and try to be as patient as I can with their needs."

We then discussed various batting styles, he'd never seen Ted Williams play, so he signed his book: "To Ceo and Geordie, May you hit like Tony Oliva (the finest he ever saw), Best wishes, Rod Carew."

I conducted three more interviews in L.A. in the weeks preceding our departure, beginning with a neighbor of mine, the great Dodger catcher, Roy Campanella. Now sixty-four and confined to a wheelchair, he and his second wife, Roxie, live down in the valley of Woodland Hills. And though he's remained a part of the Dodger Community Relations team with Don Newcombe and "Sweet Lou" Johnson, throughout our conversation in his trophy room, filled with three MVP awards, Mexican and American Hall of Fame plaques, and bronzed baseball shoes, I kept picturing him in his powerful, rotund prime, spitting on his hands when he came to bat and then, with that looping, roundhouse swing, his right knee dipping low, whacking the ball high, unbelievably high, into those cozy Ebbets Field stands as he went jogging around the bases with his belly jiggling before him, or, amazingly catlike behind the plate, whipping bulletlike throws to nail stealing or straying base runners.

"Roy, you remember a game in St. Louis, Preacher

Roe was pitching, and the Cardinals got about twelve hits or so, but you kept picking them off base, so that the Dodgers won, 2–1?"

"I remember a game against the Cardinals I picked two men off second base in the same inning."

"Right, that was it—and it was incredible! Anyway, did your father play sports?"

"No, my dad never played sports. Though he never minded me playin', just told me to be home when I was supposed to be home when I played around the neighborhood and in school."

"As you developed as a player, did he encourage you to be a professional?"

"Well at that time now, no black player was in the major leagues and I had planned, once I had gotten into junior high school—say the eighth grade—to be a draftsman, I wanted to be an architect. I never had the slightest idea I had the ability or even *thought* about playin' in the major leagues, because there was nothin' to think about then, till my physical education teacher in the ninth grade asked me why didn't I go out for the baseball team. And I told him I had never thought about it, I played football, basketball, I was on the track and field team, I ran the hundred-yard dash. So I reported to the gymnasium that one afternoon and they had circles for infielders, outfielders, pitchers, and catchers, and nobody went in the catcher's circle—so I went in there, and that got me started."

"How did you make the switch from architecture to baseball?"

"Oh, I was still interested in that, until a professional team in the Negro National League, the Baltimore Elite Giants, sent their owner and traveling secretary to my mother and father's house in Philadelphia. They asked my parents if they would let me play with them on the weekends. See, you couldn't play baseball in Philadelphia on Sunday, and being a Baptist, I had to go to church every Sunday. This was in 1937 and I was fifteen. But my parents said no, that I had to go to church and couldn't play no baseball on Sunday. Well, anyhow, they came back again and they sat down and offered my parents some money. And it wound up that I was able to play on the weekend if they got me back to go to school Monday morning. And I played with them through 1945. But there was two years in the summer, '43 and '44, I played in the Mexican League, when they were takin' players from the major leagues like Sal Maglie, Danny Gardella, Max Lanier, Mickey Owen. And that was the first time I played against big league players. None were on my team, I was on Monterrey, and I played with all the outsiders, Cubans and Venezuelans, I was the only American on the team—and we won the championship."

"What was your father's reaction during this time?"

"Oh, very good. My dad enjoyed it. Of course, my sisters wanted me to stay in school and go to college, because they kept tellin' my parents I had no future in baseball."

"In '45, did you think there was any chance of a black player breaking into the major leagues?"

"No, never anticipated it. Couldn't. I had no reason to. But once, after the '45 season, I played on a Negro All-Star team and we played a major league All-Star team in Ruppert Stadium in Newark, New Jersey, one night. Charlie Dressen, the coach of the Brooklyn Dodgers, was the manager of this team. And the night before that game, Jackie Robinson told me he had been over to the Dodgers' office and signed a minor league contract with Montreal for the next season. So, after the game, Charlie Dressen asked me would I come over to the Dodgers' office that Saturday mornin' at ten o'clock. And I told him yeah—I said I might have a hard time findin' it on the subway, but I'll get over there. I went into Mr. Rickey's office and he had a book on his desk about three inches thick and he read everything where they had been scouting me, they knew everything about my parents, my schoolin', what type of student I was, he had it right in this book—they had been scouting me all the time and I didn't know it."

"How about Roy, Jr.? Did you encourage him to play sports?"

"I didn't encourage him, but he was into Little League, he played in high school, but I told him when he went to Harvard that I wasn't sendin' him to Harvard to get no degree in baseball. And I told him if he didn't wanna play there, don't play. He even said, 'Dad, the studies are very tough here, I don't think I'm going to go out for any of the teams.' I said, 'That's all right with me, as long as you get your degree,' and he did. He was a very good student."

"Looking back now, do you have any regrets about your life as a ballplayer?"

"Not one. The only regret I have is the accident of running into that pole. I wouldn't try that again."

Roy Campanella, Jr., is a smaller, thirty-eight-year-old, bespectacled version of his father, but with the same rotund build, a warm and intelligent single parent of two children, fifteen-year-old Roy III and fourteen-year-old Akua. A writer, producer, and director, he's worked on most of TV's major sitcoms. The boys and I met him on the Burbank Studios lot that same afternoon, where he was directing an episode of *Hotel,* and he talked freely about his childhood.

"Well, my dad didn't encourage me to play professionally, that's true, but obviously with baseball being such a big part of his life, my interest in it was just natural, so as a youngster I enjoyed playing an awful lot and going out to the ball park, but it always seemed to be *his* profession, and I was drawn, really, to motion pictures and television production. I perfectly understood he had a very busy schedule and not being able to be at a lot of my games—I didn't go through any kind of traumatic thing over that—I mean, my God, how's my father gonna come to a Little League game if he's got to play a major league game?"

"Did your mother help in your understanding of this?"

"Oh, sure, my mother was very understanding. She was very athletic, and, in fact, played on a women's basketball team in the World's Fair of 1939. She played tennis with Althea Gibson, they grew up together in Harlem and were tennis buddies."

"Where did you grow up?"

"In Glen Cove, and it was a very comfortable, upper-middle-class existence on the North Shore of Long Island."

"What were you praised for as a child by your father?"

"Well, he liked the way I played football, he liked the way I played baseball. He thought I could play professionally, but I mean it wasn't like he said, 'Hey, you oughta be a ballplayer' or 'Hey, you *have* to do that.' It was more a passing thought kind of thing."

"How old were you when your father had the accident, and what memories do you have of it?"

"I was ten and it was a devastating blow, probably one of the most traumatic periods of my life. My mother handled it very well and did an excellent job in explaining the situation to us."

"Finally, what was it like being the son of a legend?"

"Well, it had a lot of weight, and also, being the second or junior, I tended to emphasize my first name as a kid, so that other children, my peers, would have a chance to respond to me as me, or as just 'Roy.' You get a lotta kids who feel that you obviously have to be stuck-up or narcissistic, who assume automatically that you feel better than them, so they test you, and then they get to know you and they say, 'Oh, well he's not like that, he's a real good guy.' "

Next day we drove out to Dodger Stadium, that Baskin-Robbins of a ball park with its pastel candy-cane colors, high atop Chavez Ravine. Arriving well before game time, there were few people about as we roamed throughout the orange and blue seats and were suddenly struck, after all those spring training bandboxes, by the sheer size of these major league surroundings: hundreds of straw-hatted vendors, security guards with walkie-talkies, plush press facilities—and that continuing fantasy image of three and two, bottom of the ninth, and 50,000 fans screaming at the top of their lungs as Geordie smiling, gave the play-by-play call: "A high drive into deep left field, Guerrero going back, a way back, to the track, to the wall—it's gone! Wimmer's belted another one!"

From behind home plate, in the prestigious field-level boxes regularly used by Cary Grant and Doris Day, we watched the Dodger pitchers take their batting practice cuts, joshing and betting each other who'd hit the most out—Fernando far and away the best slugger, smacking four in the short time we saw him—before I moved inside, toward the Braves' clubhouse and my meeting with Dale Murphy.

I was well aware of his clean-cut, All-American-boy image, that he'd won the 1985 Lou Gehrig Memorial Award, given to the player most exemplifying the character of that Hall of Famer, attended Brigham Young University, married a blond cheerleader there, and had four sons, ages six, three, two, and nine months. His former manager Joe Torre had said, "If you're a coach, you want him as a player. If you're a father, you want him as a son. If you're a woman, you want him as a husband. If you're a kid, you want him as a father." But I'd also learned of other factors in his life. His second son, Travis, was born with Rubinstein-Taybi Syndrome, a rare disease that retards mental and physical development, inverts thumbs, and causes epicanthic folds in the eyelids, giving the face and nose a flatness. Three and a half, he'd been making slow, steady progress, and Dale wasn't worried. "We believe we are all put on this earth to be tested," he'd said, "but a child like Travis, we believe, has already passed the test."

And there he was, a gentle giant with his fresh, boyish face and enormous hands, a jolly lifeguard looking me right in the eye with a smile and nearly always stressing the positive.

"Did your father play sports?"

"Well I'm not exactly sure as far as collegiate athletics,

I think he was involved a little bit, but I never saw any letters or anything. His favorite sport was golf. He's an electrical engineer by profession in Portland, Oregon."

"Did he encourage you to play baseball?"

"Well he always gave me the opportunity, didn't do anything more than say, 'Hey, Little League's startin', you know, it's time to go,' so I never really felt like I was in a pushing type situation, but always felt encouragement. My first year, when I was eight, I got one hit the whole season."

"Well that gives hope to all Little Leaguers."

Laughing, he added, "I know, I didn't start out too well. But I never really felt like that was bad, nobody made a big deal about it, and I think that helps, because, really, who else remembers that I got one hit except me?"

"You remember what that hit was?"

"Oh, no, I have no idea. It was probably an error," and he laughed again, "and I thought it was a hit."

"Have you encouraged your boys to play?"

"Well our oldest is six, and they start T-ball so young, so we only have one involved right now. But he likes it, and if he wants to go out there, we'll give him that opportunity. I think it's a little young basically, they really don't know how to catch and throw."

"Is it tough for him as a ballplayer being your son?"

"In some respects. He probably hasn't noticed it yet, but I've noticed and heard certain things. You know, it bothered me a little bit, people come over to watch him hit, but it's something you have to live with, I guess. We just teach our kids that people react that way 'cause I'm a ballplayer, but we're not any different than anyone else."

We then got onto the topic of ballplayers being coached ever since they could walk, manager after manager, and of a willingness not only to follow orders, but, my contention, of a *need* to follow orders. I wondered if he agreed.

"Well as an athlete that's just part of your life. In high school, you do what the coach says or you're off the team, you don't play. Here, you can be a little more critical 'cause it is a job and you can question why a manager is doin' this or doin' that, but if he tells me to do it and I don't agree with him, I've still gotta do it. You know, I might ask him afterward, why did you do such and such? Whereas in high school, I would never ever go up to him and ask. But yeah, it's just part of your training."

"Do you see it as sort of not growing up?"

"Oh, sure, I don't think any of us have really grown up because, like you say, we've been doin' the same thing since we were eight years old. And I think that's why some athletes tend to have a few problems, 'cause we haven't grown up and we're immature and we're sheltered and we're pampered and we don't know what it's like to work for a living. And a lot of people won't look at that as a detrimental part of the game, but it certainly is, 'cause we don't know what it's like livin' in the real world, and that can be really frightening after you retire."

"Would you like your sons to become professional ballplayers?"

"Well I don't have any strong feeling about that either way. If they want to, that's fine. I'm gonna try and encourage 'em in whatever they wanna do. There's a certain amount of obsession with the game professionally, and I'm convinced that obsession is not healthy no matter what you're involved with. But you've almost gotta be that way to a certain degree. A baseball life is so short, and there're so many more important things than this, that you've gotta be careful. But the problem is people pamper you, give you so much, you make the money, you come out here and people clap for you, cheer for you, and you *get* obsessed with it to the point of you can't quit, it's why guys hang on. You can't adjust to a normal life, your family suffers, and so you gotta be careful. But you also can't be nonchalant and say, 'This ain't any big deal,' because, hey, look at the amount of people who've been able to *do* it, how few? So I try to find that happy medium. But it's tough."

"How about when it's over? What would you like to do?"

"I'm not sure yet. I know one thing I'd like is to go to a game with all of my kids and sit in the upper deck.

I really look forward to that day when we can come to the ball park just like everyone else and watch together as a family—that'd be fun. What's frustrating now is you don't feel like you ever have enough time with 'em, and it goes by so fast."

Ted Williams, 1965 (photograph by Robert Riger)

The author and Williams, 1986 (Wimmer private collection)

Yaz in his prime (UPI-Bettmann Newsphotos)

The author and
John Henry Wil-
liams at Winter
Haven (Wimmer
private collection)

Williams watches
John Henry as
George Scott look
on. (Wimmer
private collection)

Ceo at the plate
(Wimmer private
collection)

'ade Boggs at Winter Haven (Wimmer
rivate collection)

Stan Musial in modest attire
(National Baseball Library,
Cooperstown, NY)

The Wizard of Oz (National Baseball Library, Cooperstown, NY)

Geordie at Al Lang Field, Ozzie Smith behind (Wimmer private collection)

Richie Ashburn (National Baseball Library, Cooperstown, NY)

The author and Ashburn in the Phillies press box, 1986
(Wimmer private collection)

Mike Schmidt and Geordie
(Wimmer private collection)

George Kell (National Baseball
Library, Cooperstown, NY)

Vin Scully and the author at Vero Beach
(Wimmer private collection)

Orel Hershiser being interviewed (Wimmer private collection)

Sandy Koufax and Tommy Lasorda at Vero, 1986
(Los Angeles Dodgers photo)

Joe DiMaggio and Mickey Mantle at an Old Timers' Game
(UPI-Bettmann Newsphotos)

l Ripken, Sr.'s lonesome cowboy
k (National Baseball Library,
operstown, NY)

The grin of Cal Ripken, Jr.
(National Baseball Library,
Cooperstown, NY)

Rod Carew as a Twin
(National Baseball Library,
Cooperstown, NY)

Roy Campanella (National Baseball
Library, Cooperstown, NY)

Roy Campanella and his son, 1986 (photograph by Neal Preston)

Ceo at Wrigley Field (Wimmer private collection)

All-American Dale Murphy (National Baseball Library, Cooperstown, NY)

Ron Santo with Rusty Staub sliding in (National Baseball Library, Cooperstown, NY)

Steve Garvey (National Baseball Library, Cooperstown, NY)

Tony Gwynn (National Baseball Library, Cooperstown, NY)

Lou Boudreau as a broadcaster (Wimmer private collection)

The youthful Lou Boudreau (National Baseball Library, Cooperstown, NY)

The sweet swing
of George Brett
(National Baseball
Library,
Cooperstown, NY)

father and son at the Hall of Fame (Wimmer private collection)

Gary Carter's toothy
Pepsodent smile
(National Baseball
Library,
Cooperstown, NY)

Don Mattingly (National Baseball Library, Cooperstown, NY)

Hal Richman with his son, Adam, and Strat-O-Matic
(Wimmer private collection)

Earl Weaver (National Baseball Library, Cooperstown, NY)

Reggie Jackson unloading (National Baseball Library, Cooperstown, NY)

Eric Davis and his father, Jimmy (Wimmer private collection)

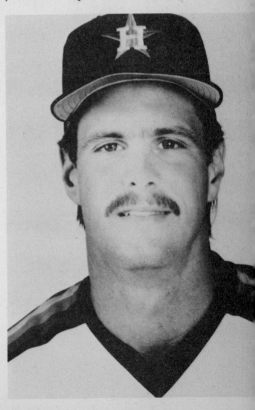

Glenn Davis (National Baseball
Library, Cooperstown, NY)

Yogi Berra (National Baseball Library, Cooperstown, NY)

# Chapter Eight

**J**uly 20 was upon us in a dazzling flash of L.A. sun and me anxiously pacing around the United Airlines lounge, trying to remember what I'd left behind—when I abruptly bumped into Ceo and glanced up into his eyes.

"God, you got so big!"

"He's taller than you, Dad," said Geordie.

"No way."

And we stood back to back while he measured us with his hand and found, to my surprise and Ceo's guilty delight, that indeed it was true that my older son had grown now to six feet one.

Then off to Chicago we flew on a bumpy four-hour flight—marveling, as Murphy said, at how fast the years go by—and next morning, we were driving for the first time ever through the leafy North Side toward the friendly confines of Wrigley Field at the corner of Clark and Addison. We parked in the VIP lot, were let in early, and, dream of dreams for the wide-eyed fan, had the ball park all to ourselves. The boys free to run unimpeded up and down the aisles and under the tin-roofed stands, above the shaggy vines and mellow brick and out to the center-field, manually-operated scoreboard. The Lake Michigan winds kept blowing gustily

113

in and, later on, home runs went sailing straight into the bleachers and their waiting hands—as though the Cubs, giving a command performance, were taking batting practice just for them!

Grinning, I headed up to the rickety press box for a prearranged interview with Ron Santo, the former Cub third baseman and a longtime favorite of mine. He was nineteen when he signed for $18,000, played fifteen years in the majors, slammed 342 homers, and retired in 1974. Gene Mauch had once called him the best third baseman he'd ever seen over an extended period. "Billy Cox and Frank Malzone may have been good for one season, but they can't match Santo over ten years." Now forty-six, Ron currently runs Interpoint, a company that operates Union 76 truck stops throughout the United States, and he still lives in Chicago with his second wife, Vicki.

I began, as usual, asking if his father played sports.

"My father, my real father, played softball and a little handball, he was a pretty good athlete. But my father —it's kind of a different story—my real father left when I was like six years old, but he put a glove in my hand when I was like two years old. But I never saw him again until I was nineteen. Actually, my stepfather had a lot more to do with my professional career, because he's the one that kinda raised me in Seattle, Washington. My mother remarried when I was twelve years old, and when I graduated high school, there was all sixteen major league teams after me, he was the one that sat down and we talked to every individual scout that came in. And he said to me, 'Son,' he says, 'whatta you wanna do, you wanna go to a major league team that's gonna give you all this money, or do you wanna make the major leagues?' And I said I wanna make the major leagues. So I signed with the Cubs for the least amount of money—in fact, probably forty to fifty thousand dollars less than I woulda got from any other ball club—but which I still think was a good decision."

"Did you play sports when you were young?"

"Sure did. I played Little League and Babe Ruth at twelve and then American Legion in my sophomore year in high school."

"Was it hard not having a father during those early years?"

"It was very difficult, very, very difficult."

"Was your real father or your stepfather critical of you in any way?"

"My stepfather was, but he'd come to every game, along with my mother, and if I went four for four, he would just mention to me that I coulda done this right. Really, there wasn't any accolades until, surprisingly enough, I graduated and then he told me how good he thought I was."

"What was it like not getting any praise?"

"Well, I guess I knew I was good, and I really didn't need it. He didn't criticize me, he never put me down, he was just trying to keep my head from gettin' too big, because I was very successful early."

"Did you encourage your sons?"

"Well, havin' a major league ballplayer for a dad, my son Ron, Jr., went through a very difficult time, because we had Ronnie when I was like twenty years old, and so he kinda grew up with me in the major leagues and he saw the ups and downs. But he was a very good Little League ballplayer, I mean you could see he had all the tools, and one day he came home and said, 'I quit, Dad,' and I said, 'Why'd you quit?' and he said, 'Well, because they expect me to be as good as you.' And this was when he was about eight or nine years old, and I said, 'Son, I understand perfectly. You do what you wanna do, it's up to you.' And he ended up goin' back, but I didn't encourage it. And he went through a lot in high school, there was times Ronnie got a lot of abuse."

"Did he play college ball?"

"He played his first year in college and then he didn't play after that. My second son, Jeff, was the opposite. The way to explain this to you is that, obviously, Ron Santo, Jr., stuck out more than Jeff Santo, and so Jeff never had that kinda pressure. He played high school ball and then he went to St. Leo's College, played ball one year there, and then left and went to Miami of Ohio and he played two years there."

"How'd you feel about them not going into professional ball?"

"Well, I felt good about it. I don't think Ronnie ever had any aspirations of bein' a major league ballplayer—

at least I don't think he did—and there was so much pressure that I was very happy that he didn't."

"How've they reacted to it? I mean, what's happened to them?"

"Oh, they're great, they're fabulous, yeah. Jeff graduated in communications from Miami of Ohio and Ronnie is working, doin' very well, and plays softball and, you know, just loves it."

"Do you see any of your father in the way you parented your kids?"

"No, 'cause I never had a father. I hadda stepfather that I loved very much. He and my mother were killed in 1974 in a car wreck comin' down to spring training my last year. And my real father's still alive, but I don't see him."

"Any reason why not?"

"Yeah, there's *my* reasons, the fact that he left when I was six years old and never showed up again till I was nineteen and I was in the big leagues. And I was mad— I *been* mad for a long time."

"Did you find many absent fathers in the major leagues?"

"You know, I never thought about it, but it's a good point, it's very common, very definitely. It's funny, but that's very true."

My own boys were still frolicking joyously about in the bleachers, so I made my way down to the Padres' clubhouse, a rather compact cubicle, to talk to Steve

Garvey—whose replies all sounded as though they were being read from a prepared text as he beetled his brows below his slick black hair and crossed his Popeye forearms. His father had been a first baseman at a parochial high school in Hempstead, Long Island, worked for Greyhound, and, later, drove the Dodgers' spring training bus for The Boys of Summer.

"Well, I think Dad really took what I call a perfect approach. He introduced me to sports, baseball first, allowed me to develop my own interests, encouraged me once I sought to participate in a sport, provided the best equipment he could afford, and then just tried to make the practices and see all the games."

Tony Gwynn passed by with a grin, and his lower lip stretched full of Red Man chaw. I followed him up the narrow ramp and into the Padres' dugout with its polished pine seats, white concrete ceiling touching the top of my head, and chatted for a while about hitting with this articulate, easygoing man, who'd read Williams' book but felt it didn't really apply to him.

"How 'bout 'hips in front of hands'?"

"Oh that's true. Even though I hit the ball the other way a lot, it's the hips-and-hands kind of motion that gets it there."

"Any heroes growing up?"

"Willie Davis, still the fastest man I ever saw."

Two old-timers, reporters from small midwestern papers, now wedged themselves beside me and began to reminisce. The older one, who'd just turned seventy-five, told me of seeing Babe Ruth slice a pop-fly double into the left-field corner during the '32 Series. I asked him had he ever seen Ted Williams. "Oh sure." "When?" "In the All-Star Game, 1962. Yeah, right here it was." "Williams retired in 1960." "Oh. . . ."

But baseball, of course, can do that to you, blurring years and players and moments into a confusion of slow-motion dreamscapes. And especially here, I thought, as I strolled lazily onto the field and gazed around those ancient confines where my kids waved and continued to play, and where the grass and lighting were still natural. For baseball, as Ernie Banks once said, "is a personal game, meant for small parks such as this. You've got to feel close, get involved. The fans would sleep here if they could. And so would I."

Behind the batting cage, I talked for a bit with Billy Williams and Ryne "the Devine" Sandberg, then joined the boys in the stands as the game began. The Cubs were going with a rookie left-hander, Jamie Moyer, against the Padres' LaMarr (or "Druggie," as Geordie called him) Hoyt. Riffling through the program, I found an article about how many current players were sons of former minor leaguers: Cal Ripken, Jr., Frank Tanana, Rollie Fingers, Mark Gubicza, Ron Hassey, Mike Flanagan, Brian Giles, Dave Righetti, and Dennis "Oil Can" Boyd. But that absent from any big league rosters were such sons as Joe DiMaggio, Jr., Jackie Robinson, Jr., Hank Aaron, Jr., and all three of Ty Cobb's boys. Ty Cobb, Jr., I remembered reading, was a major disappointment to his father, disliking baseball and taking up tennis. He flunked out of Princeton, then went to Yale, where he captained the varsity tennis team, but never received his bachelor's degree. Eventually, he and his father became totally alienated from each other, which Cobb always blamed on the boy's mother.

The Padres failed to score in the top of the first as the loudly booed Garvey closed it out, to the delirium of the Cub faithful, by grounding into a fast 4-6-3 double play turned by the flamboyantly fielding, rocket-armed shortstop Shawon Dunston, who then led off the bottom of the inning with a kangaroo-hop chopper over third for a double and, two outs later, scooted home with the opening run. This same Dunston, the *Media Guide* informed me, had hit .790 during his senior year at New York's Thomas Jefferson High School. Chicago added two more in the sixth as Geordie continued to fill in his scorecard. The crowd kept up a noisy, partisan clamor with a Dixieland band clanging out "The Sidewalks of New York" and a seeming horde of vendors hawking David Berg hot dogs, Pepsi, and "Old-style" beer. I'd never seen so many vendors, one of them telling me that he and 140 others were "just selling beer alone." But why so many? "Because we're the best-paid in the majors." And glancing around the ball park, I became aware what a predominately white crowd this was as I spotted only one or two black faces here and there throughout the stands.

During the seventh-inning stretch, Harry Caray led

us all in a sing-along of "Take Me Out to the Ball Game" from his tinny WGN broadcast booth above (later in the year, during a fourteen-inning game, he was to do it twice). And, shortly thereafter, the Cubbies put it on ice, tallying three runs in the eighth as they coasted to a 6-1 win and the blue flag flew flapping out in center field.

But we weren't quite through yet as we hustled back along the rickety catwalks to the WGN booth for an interview with another favorite of mine, former Cleveland shortstop and Hall of Famer Lou Boudreau, who'd been broadcasting Cub games for nearly thirty years. Having just celebrated his sixty-ninth birthday, he looked somehow sad and bewildered with his grizzled hair and glasses, like an aged tiger at the zoo. But he was still the boy-manager in my mind as I recalled my father and me at Yankee Stadium in 1949 watching one of the first games I ever saw: Yogi Berra drilling a sharp single into left-center field, Rizzuto on his way to third, Boudreau cutting off the relay and, without even looking, whirling and rifling his throw back to first to nail Berra taking a wide turn around the bag.

"Did your father play sports?"

"Yes, my father was a semipro third baseman, played around Kankakee and Momence, Illinois, Blue Island and Harvey. And he was the one who changed me from a catcher to a third baseman, would take me out in the afternoons and hit me ground balls from the age of six right on up till I entered high school and college. He would always try to instill in me to be aggressive and try to break a record every day, would keep score as to how many I could field in a row without an error. There weren't Little Leagues in those days, so we would play corner baseball a lot, right on the street corners."

"Did you encourage your sons?"

"Yes, I tried to encourage them to do what they wanted to—of course, they would make up their own minds. When they took to baseball, then, of course, I was 100 percent behind them, tried to push them into it somewhat. One of them is playing professional ball with Charlotte now in the Baltimore organization, he's a left-handed pitcher. And the other one is in the advertising business in Phoenix, Arizona."

"Was it hard for them to follow a legend?"

"It was for my older son. It happened close to the end of my playing career and I thought it was unfair for a lot of sportswriters and sportscasters to try to compare him with me. I was fortunate enough to have great years and become a Hall of Famer, and it put a lot of pressure on him."

"Were you critical in any way of your sons?"

"No, no, I tried to keep that within myself, kept praying and hoping that they could make the grade but hoping that still I wasn't being too critical so as to stop them from trying. As long as they tried and performed at their best and gave out effort, that's all I asked."

"Any regrets playing baseball?"

"Very few, I was very fortunate. I became a player, I became a manager, youngest playing manager in the game of baseball, I became a Most Valuable Player, I led the league in batting, I led the league eight consecutive years in fielding, I made five All-Star teams, I managed one All-Star team, I played in the World Series, I won a World Series, so I was very fortunate."

"Since you'll always be associated with the 'Williams Shift,' one final question: Was he the best hitter you ever saw?"

"Yes, no doubt about it. I did not see as much of Musial as I did of Williams, and a lot of National League people will tell you in those days that Musial was as great as Williams. When I put on the 'Williams Shift,' I knew he could go to left field, but I knew what type of individual he was, and, after talking with him, I knew he wanted a challenge. And he got the challenge from me and he tried to hit through it. And we found ourselves 35 percent better off in retiring him."

"If you hadn't put the 'Shift' on, what do you think he would've hit?"

".400 again. Oh, I'd say he would've hit it two out of three years, two out of five years."

"How did you come up with the 'shift'?"

"Well he was beating me so much in 1946, it happened on the first game of a doubleheader, I was fortunate to tie a major league record by getting five extra-base hits in nine innings with four doubles and a home run, and with three swings of the bat, he hit three home runs and drove in eight runs. So here he was joggin' around the bases, and I was wearin' myself out tryin' to get a double. And I was angry at the time, and had been thinking about it for several weeks, and my coaches said it cannot be done, you can't do it, and finally this particular day I was upset and stubborn in the second game of a doubleheader, we had two out, and when Williams came up, I just yelled, 'Yo!' (I had a meeting between the games and told 'em what we were gonna do, and the ball club laughed, of course, and said if that's what you want, we'll do it.) So after I yelled 'Yo!,' they all moved over to the positions that I had diagramed on the bulletin board, and Williams just stepped out of the batter's box, leaned on the bat, and told the umpire to get the S.O.B.'s back in their positions. And Bill Sommers was the umpire and he told him, 'Ted, as long as they're within the foul lines and not in the stands, they're OK.' So Williams then twisted that bat—he used to really twist that bat till sawdust came out of it—because now he wanted to hit against the 'Shift.' "

"And what'd he do, first time up?"

"He hit a line drive on one hop to my second baseman, who was playing in short right field, it was a sinking line drive, and he threw him out."

We all shook hands and left the broadcast booth as I followed the boys along the rickety catwalks toward the ramp, slowing my pace, mincing forward, not looking down. I was remembering my father's impatience years ago, striding before me in Yankee Stadium, "Come on, come on, nothing to be scared of up here," and

Geordie, well aware of my fear of heights, now shaking his head and saying, "Dad, you're paranoid!"

"Wrong word," I mumbled and edged nervously on.

"Whatever."

Ceo joining his brother, "So lame, Dad!"

Later that night, we saw *Ferris Bueller's Day Off*, and the boys, excited at recognizing all the Chicago landmarks, decided that tomorrow they'd go to the top of the Sears Tower, the world's tallest building. They wanted me to join them, but I, of course, refused.

Though the following afternoon, when they returned with the usual razzing—"Dad, you would've gone crazy!" said Geordie on his way to the bathroom—Ceo, softening, asked, "Dad, *why're* you so scared? You shouldn't be." He then confessed that he'd been frightened, too, when they'd reached the top. "But I overcame my fear by forcing myself to look down, just like Ferris Bueller."

# Chapter Nine

**A**nd jogging out of the Calabasas dugout for the bottom of the fourth, I smile as I think of that moment again, of role reversals, letting kids walk away, and of the comments of forty-year-old Kansas City Royals outfielder Hal McRae, who, with his nineteen-year-old son Brian, could possibly be the first father and son to play together on the same team in the majors. "You can't impart all your knowledge, even to your son, because there's so much a person has to learn for himself. It's not important that Brian hit the way I do; in fact, he shouldn't. It's important for him to be Brian and me to be Hal."

And for Geordie to be Geordie, of course, as he disdains the bunt once more and slaps a sharp single up the middle to give the JV a 5-0 lead. Ceo, meanwhile, with the varsity locked in a 1-1 tie, walks, steals second, and, as he later will say about his second at-bat, "trying to pull an outside pitch rather than take it to left," whacks a hot shot, but right at the first baseman, his hips going one way and his head another.

# Chapter Ten

**N**ext day, we drove east out of Chicago, up through the scraggly drabness of northern Indiana, past the dark Michigan woods to the lovely college town of Ann Arbor. Back in June, a Hollywood producer, thinking our adventure might make a good TV movie, suggested a possible fictional plot where along the way Ceo would meet a girl and I would meet a girl, and I laughed. "Why're you laughing?" she asked. "Because my son's so shy right now, no way would he ever meet a girl, except in a script."

When we arrived at the Sheraton University Inn, I confirmed our tickets for the Royals-Tigers game the following night and my interview with George Brett, and, just before dinner, the boys decided they were going for a swim and a jacuzzi in the motel pool while I took a nap. But five minutes later, Geordie came tearing back through the door: "Dad, listen-listen, you won't believe what just happened! OK, we're going down the corridor and these two girls're walking by, both looking like Shamu the Whale and one of them says to Ceo, 'She (meaning her friend) wants to go to bed with you!' "

"What? Come on, here in Ann Arbor? Who *are* they?"

"I don't know, high school girls, 'bout sixteen."

"And what'd Ceo do?"

"Nothing, nothing! You know Ceo, he just kept walking, head down, into the pool."

"Then what happened?"

"I don't know, 'cause I came back to tell you."

An hour later, Ceo returned and, smiling his shy, innocent smile, described what happened next. The pool was filled, so he went in the empty jacuzzi and, as soon as he jumped in, ten girls jumped in after him. Geordie asked if they were all "Sumos," and Ceo laughed. "Yeah, and they'd never met anyone from L.A., wanted to know if *I* was from L.A. Have I met any movie stars? And when I told 'em I met the Fonz, they started going crazy! 'Oh my God, you met the Fonz, you met the Fonz?'"

"And they're all fat?"

Ceo laughed again. "Yeah, all dorkos, Shamus."

"Dad, didn't I tell you?"

"Oh, one wasn't bad, sort of pretty, but she walked kinda funny, like all hunched over."

Geordie then chimed in, "I bet I know where she's going to college."

"Where?" I asked.

"Notre Dame."

But that night after dinner, Ceo went for another "swim" alone, and when he returned, informed us he was going out for the evening.

"With Quasimodo?"

"Geordie!"

"No, another one—"

"But I thought they were all 'Shamus'?"

"Well not all, one's—"

"Oh, I know who she is, the one who looks like Ally Sheedy, right, right?"

"Yeah, sort of. Anyway, we're all goin' out, be back later."

"Going out where?"

"I don't know. There's this party up in their room."

"Are you the only boy?"

"I don't know. I think so."

"And what time'll you be back?"

"Dad, I don't know."

He came back once at ten for money and the car keys and to tell me they were all going to *The Rocky Horror Show.*

"Who's 'all'?"

"Ally?"

"What's her name?"

"Meredith, and her father teaches at Michigan State. Dad, come on, I gotta go, lemme have the car keys!"

"Who else is going?"

"Her and her friend."

"*She* and her friend."

"She and her friend."

"The *three* of you?"

"Yeah." I tossed him the keys. "See ya later, thanks, bye-bye," and he took off like a shot.

And stayed out all night. He shyly explained the next morning, or afternoon, when he finally awoke, that the three of them—he, Meredith, and Shamu—went to the movie, had a Burger King breakfast at 7:00 A.M., and then, totally exhausted, came home.

Early that evening, we drove into Detroit, with Ceo, still groggy, spread across the backseat. And though I'd never been to this city, I'd certainly read about its economic conditions as Tiger Stadium appeared shimmering in the distance and we pulled off the ramp, continuing to cruise through a surrounding landscape of incredible and seemingly never-ending poverty, walled-up storefronts or buildings falling to ruin like a bombed-out war zone. We paused briefly for lunch at a black-owned Hardee's, then went on foot into a once rather posh neighborhood, genteel homes with pillared porches and verandas, but that was now crumbling and garbage-littered.

I told the boys, as we drove along, of some recent articles I'd read in *Time* and *The Atlantic* on the Underclass: that half of America's black children live in families with incomes below the poverty line, 80 percent of which are headed by females; that the high school dropout rate was as great as 89 percent; and that the chance of a criminal getting away with a crime within the urban ghettos, assuming he was not a murderer or a rapist, was thought by the police to be between 90 and 95 percent.

Outside our car windows were not the unemployed but the unemployable. And contrary to popular myth, this was no longer the breeding ground for future professional athletes. These men and boys, passing or standing idly by, had mostly quit school and would never graduate. No Darryl Strawberrys from L.A.'s Crenshaw High nor Dwight Goodens from Tampa's Hillsborough here. Sport, for those out there on the streets, if they still played and drugs hadn't yet claimed them, was for themselves, one-on-one games without control or formal coaching.

And at Tiger Stadium that night, the impact was even more profound. For again, as in Chicago, looking around, there was a 95 percent white crowd within that glittering ball park, the most beautiful we'd seen so far, with its glossy blue and orange seats and symmetrical tiers—like a jewel in a sea of poverty. There were many white fathers and white sons, but few if any black fathers with their sons. In 1986, baseball was still a white man's game, as opposed to basketball, and as evidenced by two thirds of the players on the field that night for both the Tigers and the Royals.

Denied press passes, the boys took their complimentary seats fifteen rows back of home plate, and I moved inside toward the Kansas City clubhouse and my meeting with George Brett. I'd always admired him as a hitter, and especially when he blasted a 95-mile-per-hour Goose Gossage fast ball into Yankee Stadium's upper-right-field deck in the 1980 American League playoffs, capping an astonishing .390 season.

But more than that, I'd become intrigued with his background after reading a recent copy of Geordie's *Sporting News* about his three older brothers and strange father, who'd never attended the World Series nor ever been to one of George's thirty playoff games. Instead, Jack Brett stayed at his Manhattan Beach, California, home and watched on TV or listened on the radio. A finance director for a company associated with Nissan, he was quoted as saying, "You can't get too close to your sons," admitting he was sort of stoic. "I think that with a friendly look, a little smile, and nodding your head, you can show your affection. If he hit four hundred homers in a row, I would not say anything to him. I would not say anything to anyone. I would just nod my head. I make it a point never to talk about George. Never. My attitude is, 'He had a great game, but he was lucky.' " All of Brett's brothers had played professional baseball: John, thirty-nine, now a general contractor, dropped out after hitting .088 in the Midwest League in 1968; Bobby, thirty-four, hit .286 at Billings in the Pioneer League in 1972, one year after George made his professional debut there; and Ken, thirty-eight, hung on with ten teams for fourteen years in the majors, compiling an 83-85 won-lost record with a 3.93 ERA and a .262 lifetime batting average.

As the youngest of the four, George, thirty-two, was considered the least likely to succeed by his father, who'd remained a strict disciplinarian as his son still strove for acceptance. He'd given all ten of his All-Star rings to his father, brought him to Kansas City to be present when he signed his lifetime contract, and called him the night he homered off Gossage.

This season he'd started slowly, plagued by nagging

injuries, and I found him anxious and ill at ease during the interview, his gaze shifting, always looking askance when he answered or gnawing away on a big chaw in his mouth. His father had never played sports, at least as far as he knew, though he thought everything that'd been said about them "had been blown so far out of proportion, it's crazy. We had a good relationship when I was growing up, it wasn't goin' out in the backyard and playin' catch with your son—I had three older brothers—and it was hard for him to devote time to me because of them."

"Were you always thinking of a baseball career?"

"No, not really. My goal was to be a football player, I wanted to be a quarterback for the New York Jets. That was my ultimate dream, played four years of high school football, sometimes at quarterback, sometimes at wide receiver. But I wasn't a very good quarterback, I didn't get any college scholarships, and I got drafted by the Royals, so I decided to play baseball."

"Was your father critical of you in any way?"

"Very. Very comparative, always compared me to my brothers and always compared all of us to one another in sports. And very critical, yeah. You do good, you could play with them, you do bad, he would let you know you did bad. He gave you a lotta drive, gave you a lotta incentive."

"Looking back, how do you feel about that?"

"I think I needed it. I think I still need it. And that's why he still gives it to me."

"I asked Mike Schmidt was his father ever critical of him, and he said in everything he did. If he hit two home runs at Riverfront, his father wouldn't bat an eye. Does that sound similar?"

Brett nodded and kept looking off, "Uh-hum, yeah."

"Any regrets about being a ballplayer, things you might've missed in life?"

"No, I don't think so. I made a decision when I was eighteen years old to play professional baseball, and you make a decision like that, you can't look back on it. I just try to give everything I can for as long as I can, and then when my career is over, then I can say, 'Well maybe it wasn't the right thing to do.' But right now, I'm very happy and pleased with what I decided."

"If you hadn't played ball, what would you have done?"

"Oh, I don't know, I have no idea, I woulda went to school probably and played baseball in college, and then who knows what would've happened from there."

"When it's over, do you have any idea what you'll do?"

"I'm gonna be vice president of the Royals for seven years, and then I don't know what I'm gonna do."

"Are you looking forward to having sons of your own?"

"Yeah, I'd like to."

"You think you'll follow your father's parenting?"

"Uh-hum. I look at me and my brothers and I think he's done a good job raisin' all of us. I see what they've accomplished, they're all outta jail, no one's ever got in really serious trouble, they're all successful businesspeople and they're all a pleasure to be around—so I think my father did a great job raisin' all of us."

I thanked him and walked across to the Tigers' clubhouse, where Kirk Gibson and Jack Morris were playing pranks on various teammates in the shower and then giggling together like mischievous little kids as they bragged of their exploits to Lance Parrish. All of it seemed similar to high school and college shenanigans of mine, except these guys were now in their late twenties and early thirties and making a zillion dollars a season. I chatted for a while with Parrish, a gentle giant, who'd spurned a UCLA football scholarship to sign with the Tigers, and, I was surprised to find, had been Tina Turner's bodyguard for one night when she appeared on *Hollywood Squares*. He was quick to add that "it'd been blown way out of proportion, actually no big deal, a friend asked me to do it, and they made it sound like I went on tour!"

The game itself was a one-sided affair as the Tigers broke it open early with Gibson and Parrish smacking back-to-back homers on their way to a 9-2 win behind rookie right-hander Eric King, out of Royal High School in Simi Valley, and a Calabasas opponent every year.

Later that night, at the motel, Ceo saw Meridith one last time. She asked him for his address, admitted she was afraid of leaving her father and Michigan, and said that she thought he looked just like James Dean, same eyes and same great smile.

Next morning, we crossed into Canada, passing between miles of ripe, low-lying cornfields, with Geordie switching the radio stations back and forth from Phil Collins' ubiquitous "Invisible Touch," Peter Gabriel's "Sledgehammer," and Janet Jackson's "Nasty" to my "lamo" music, as Ceo called it, whenever I snuck in a moment or two of Sinatra's "Pennies from Heaven," "So weak, Dad!" or a passage from a Bach Brandenburg, before returning once more to hard rock, punk rock, and "She has a built-in ability."

Finally, somewhere in the Canadian wilds, I, too, began singing "their song."

"I thought you didn't like it, Dad?" said Geordie.

"It grows on you. 'She has a built-in ability. . . .' "

"Yeah?"

"Yeah what?"

"What're the next words?"

" 'Built-in ability to'—I don't know, tell me."

"I thought you knew it, Dad?"

"Just tell me."

" 'To take everything she sees.' "

" 'To take everything she sees.' . . . Yeah?"

"Dad, you want to stop at a hospital and check for Alzheimer's disease?"

"Geordie, will you come on!"

" 'And now it seems I'm falling for her—' "

Janet Jackson came on then with "Sitting in a movie show thinking nasty thoughts . . ." and Steve Winwood with "Higher Love."

On we drove past those endless fields and through the fumes of Hamilton, Ontario, with Ceo asking me about James Dean and what movies he was in, whether he was good-looking, how he died, then dozing off, and Geordie asking me again about his name:

"Dad, how come you named me 'S.'?" (as in S. Geordie Wimmer).

"You know why."

"Out of respect to your father."

"Right, it's a Jewish tradition."

"But it sounds so stupid! Why just 'S.'?"

"Like F. Scott Fitzgerald. Be great if you become a lawyer."

"But what if I don't?"

Ceo had never once criticized his name nor wanted to change it, whereas Geordie had toyed, at various stages and depending on his hero of the moment, with Teddy (Ballgame) Wimmer, Flash (for Gordon) Wimmer, and Dwight (for Gooden) Wimmer. My father, though, had been more upset with the naming of his first grandson, certain that he'd be the object of ridicule in school, and then, finding that others liked it, ultimately came to accept my shortened alternative of Keough.

Buffalo loomed ahead, bulky and massive and dunnish gray on the wide horizon, but somehow comforting, despite its drabness, like a retired old snuffling banker.

"Hey, guys, Buffalo looks cool!"

But Geordie, grumpy now from the drive, mumbled, "Looks disgusto!"

That night, while the still-drowsy Ceo slept, Geordie and I feasted on a local specialty, beef on weck, a sheaf of lean, thinly sliced roast beef piled on a gravy-soaked caraway seed roll sprinkled with pretzel salt, then raced out through the balmy dark to War Memorial Stadium, where *The Natural* was filmed. I was glad to have the time with him alone, free now from brother-bickering. And soon we were laughing together in front of that great, hulking tomb of a ball park, a crumbling relic still used by the Buffalo Bisons, as we each pictured ourselves as Roy Hobbs walloping that dramatic two-out, ninth-inning, towering drive into the stadium lights, then circling the bases under a Fourth of July shower of fireworks with the movie theme swelling to a crescendo.

Recently I'd read an interview with Redford wherein he'd talked about baseball being his "big thing as a kid":

> My father taught me how to play and the character in the film was taught by his father. The only sports hero I ever had was Ted Williams. He was hardly a model—but he sure was a great hitter. I tried to get him on the set during the filming of *The Natural*, but he couldn't be bothered—he was fishing at the time. That's why I like Ted Williams.

And I realized again that the greatest heroes for American men are not movie stars but sports stars. Theirs is a realm beyond celebrity: the true American royalty. Movie stars often see themselves as failed athletes who can only play out their fantasies in their films, however successful they are at the box office, Redford still wishing he were Williams, Nicholson, Kareem, and Stallone, Marciano.

Next morning, of course, I avoided the heights of Niagara Falls, telling the boys the story of Ed Delahanty, the Hall of Famer and .345 lifetime hitter, who fell into the Niagara River at the prime of his career.

"What year was that, Dad?"

"1903."

"You remember back then, Dad?"

On to Cornell we went, where I'd graduated in 1958, through the lush and rolling New York State farmlands with Madonna's "Papa Don't Preach" crackling over the airwaves as I regaled my sons with tales of my college days, and Ceo saying, "Dad, you know how many times you've told us that story?" and Geordie adding, "You live in the past, Dad."

And later thinking: How many stories do I have, even if I am a writer? Scott Fitzgerald said essentially two or three that we tell over and over. And apropos of him, that afternoon, while Geordie took a nap this time, Ceo and I visited Arthur Mizener, the Fitzgerald biographer and a former professor of mine. I hadn't seen him since the early sixties, but over the years he'd been an enthusiastic supporter of my work as we frequently talked and corresponded. His letters—full-paged, single-spaced critiques typed on his beloved 1923 portable—were special treasures to me, not only for the insightful comments they contained but also for the numerous baseball asides that told of him and Delmore Schwartz seeing Lefty Grove ("What a miracle he was!") pitch at Fenway: "Now there's a literature hook-up for you." He still recalled Carl Mays's submarine delivery, Billy Wambsganss making an unassisted triple play in the 1920 World Series, and Stanley Coveleski winning twenty-four games that same year—"None of whom I'm sure you remember. Ah, well the hell with it, you youngsters don't really know which end is up, anyway!"

Now retired as Mellon Professor of Humanities Emeritus, he and his lovely wife, Rosemary, spent a pleasant hour with us discussing the past, books, and baseball; and on our way back to the car, Ceo asked, "Are there any words they don't know?" We walked across the Arts quad together and, as we talked, it suddenly struck me how much he and his brother were now California boys, having been born in the East but living in the West these last ten years, and where, more than likely, they'd end up going to college, rather than the Ivy League of my past. Though ultimately, of course, it would be *their* choice.

At Cooperstown we snapped pictures of each other beside the Ted Williams statue (where he'd cried at its unveiling, "I never dreamed of having a statue next to Babe Ruth's"), found my boyhood buddy Hal Richman's Strat-O-Matic game enshrined in a basement display, then took off for Philadelphia—as the nitpicking began again, and now mainly focused at me. I was constantly reining in my temper or tamping it down, letting them get things off their chests, but my patience was fast wearing thin.

The weather had turned hot and humid, and especially so with the approach to the City of Brotherly Love, which offered only a snarl of chaotic traffic and tunnel jams as we were lost and found, then lost once more down the narrow, one-way streets and bumpy tram tracks with our danders rising, me boiling, and Ceo muttering, after insisting we go right, Geordie opting left, and I straight ahead, "OK, OK, Dad, whatever you say, I don't really care!," flinging the map behind him, and both of them sneering as we came around the same Market Street corner for the umpteenth time, "So lame, Dad!"—and that was the last straw, screeching to a stop by the curb and screaming:

"If I hear one more fucking '*lame*' outta you guys, you can *walk* home from here!!"

Silence. The two of them slapped down, stunned, staring off—or, rather, me striking out, refusing to take *their* slaps anymore, adolescent rebellion or whatever the hell it was!

We continued on with my heart pounding, eyes continually shifting to the rearview mirror in the simmering silence that followed, Geordie still downcast, Ceo gazing out the window—and, glancing up, I found myself looking into the eyes of my father, raccoon eyes, which were my own.

That night, under threatening skies, the temperature

now ninety-one and the humidity surely ninety-nine, we sat in first-base-line box seats at Veterans Stadium, a Hollywood idea of a ball park with its artificial turf and unreal jai-alai bounces, Phanavision instant replay, and penthouse suites, so far removed from the action that who even cared who's playing ("Pass the tonic, dear").

It was then that I apologized to them for blowing up before. I explained that I was well aware we were all getting on each other's nerves, cooped up together for ten days in the car, and that I was as guilty as they were. Ceo nodded, Geordie grunted his agreement, and soon we were joking and talking once more. I told them about the old Phillies, of Chuck Klein and Lefty O'Doul tattooing Baker Bowl's tin-faced right-field wall, of sharing Shibe Park with Connie Mack's A's, and where in 1941, Ted Williams, hitting .39955 on the eve of the season's final doubleheader, stayed out all night to walk the city's streets, stopping for ice cream a few times and covering well over ten miles before going four for five in the first game and two for three in the second to finish with a flourish at .406.

The game itself that night was far less dramatic, a sloppy slugfest won by the Phillies, 12-7, over the Cardinals that featured twenty-eight hits; Vince Coleman's three stolen bases (we'd never seen anyone steal second and third so fast, taking off like the rabbit on a greyhound track or Road Runner fleeing Wile E. Coyote); and Von Hayes's grand slam, a rising liner out to deep right center that had Tito Landrum sprinting back to the wall, all of us standing—and the ball for a second hanging suspended and luminous white against the metallic sheen of grayish-green air before dropping into the seats amid thunderous cheers.

Next morning we were off to New York in a steadily driving downpour, the tensions of being cooped up together in a car dramatically easing as we came speeding out of the Holland Tunnel, across Greenwich Village and the mad clash of Manhattan with the wonder and excitement of coming home again.

And Friday night we were out at Shea, looking down the barrel of a loaded gun—our seats directly behind home plate and ten feet under the backstop's netting—as Dwight Gooden swung into his chin-bridled windup, kicking his left leg high, and fired a 95-mile-per-hour rising blur—*whomp!*—into Carter's glove; Sinatra's "New York, New York" and Bill Haley's "Rock Around the Clock" raucously blaring between innings, and Ceo calling these "the greatest seats ever!" as he, Geordie, and their best friend and California buddy Claude hastily made up "K man" placards out of food box cardboard and, reading the results off the radar guns below, held up their tallies of "93," "94," and "95" to the crowd shouting around us.

Mixing a hopping fast ball and sharp-breaking curve, Geordie's hero, looking like the Gooden of old, went on to strike out six in a row as he pitched the Mets to a 3-1 rain-delayed win over the Expos. Throughout the game, LaGuardia's sonic ear-shattering roars and vibrations continued unabated with surreal-size jets (as in a third-rate space movie starring Buster Crabbe) zooming low overhead—expecting one, at least, to crash onto the playing field—and why, asked Ceo, couldn't they be rerouted? Here there were more cops and far more fights, an elderly usher told us after the game. He'd worked the Polo Grounds and Ebbets Field but had never seen anything like Shea, especially on Friday nights, when everybody seemed to be drinking.*

Again the boys weren't allowed in the clubhouse, so I made my way alone down the elevators of that gray, littered park, tawdry cousin to Dodger Stadium in design—it always gave me the impression of a huge subway stop alongside the ramps and overpasses of Flushing's valley of ashes. Waiting with the rest of the press corps to be let in, I asked several of them which Met I should interview, since I hadn't arranged anything in advance. Keith Hernandez, they said, was taboo because there were two topics he wouldn't discuss: drugs and his chil-

---

*During the World Series that fall, Roger Clemens was highly critical of the security at Shea Stadium. He claimed the players' wives were not properly protected, fireworks were thrown at them, and security guards called them loafers. "I'm not upset with the fans because only about a hundred ruin it for everyone else," said Clemens. "I'm talking about the security people and police. They don't buy a ticket. They're there to do a job and didn't do it." Clemens was particularly incensed at two officers who were laughing on the field after Red Sox traveling secretary Jack Rogers was felled with a bottle. Rogers required several stitches and missed almost two weeks of work.

dren. Like George Brett, he, too, was the youngest son, had a demanding and overbearing father right out of *The Great Santini,* and, to this day, turned to him first for hitting advice while he still struggled to cut the cord. "I've tried to pull away," Keith had said, "but he won't let me. I'd tell him, 'Dad, I'm a man. I don't want to be reliant on you for my career. Dad, I'm 28. . . . Dad, I'm 30. . . . Dad, I'm 31. . . . Dad, I'm 32; I'm a man.' But he wants to take credit. He's told me, 'You wouldn't have made it without me pushing you.' " And then he added, "You mean to tell me that of all the professional athletes in the world, all of them had a father that pushed and pushed and pushed on them? I find that hard to believe."

When I finally entered the Met clubhouse, I was a bit awed by tall, bald Darryl Strawberry, who'd just had all his hair shaved off, and Gooden was mobbed by reporters, so I chose Gary Carter—and was greeted with that toothy Pepsodent smile.

An eight-time All-Star, he was currently leading his team in home runs and RBIs, and had, he told me, two daughters and an infant son. His father had played some sandlot baseball, "though his big claim to fame was that he went to the same school as Pee Wee Reese in Kentucky. But as I was growing up in Fullerton, California, he was my manager, my coach, and he never forced us or really pushed us, but was always there to encourage us. And being my manager in Little League, I never got away with anything. I was the one that he picked on the most, I guess, but that goes without saying. Because if

I got away with anything, then things would've started to happen on the team and you just don't want that. But he never said I wasn't good enough—because I was one of those exceptional-type kids, I was big when I was young and pretty dominant in everything that I did, so, in that regard, he was always supportive, pattin' me on the back."

"Any regrets about being a ballplayer?"

"I have no regrets. The only thing I probably would've done, had I not torn the ligaments in my right knee my senior year in high school, was gone on and played major college football. I was offered a full scholarship to any college in the country, and I ended up choosing UCLA. I had signed a PAC-8 letter of intent, actually, and then about three or four days later, I signed a professional baseball contract. So as far as that goes, I loved football in high school, really that was my first love—when I was seven, I won the national Punt, Pass, and Kick competition—and I've always thought an education was important, but I feel that I've gotten a more worldly education here and amongst people than I ever would've in the classroom."

"What would you have done if you hadn't played baseball?"

"I would probably be involved in some capacity or another in sports, whether it be coaching or broadcasting. When it's over, my first desire is to get into broadcasting and maybe some acting, but we'll just have to wait'n see."

"What about your twenty-one-month-old son?"

"I haven't really encouraged him at this point. I mean, he picks a bat up and swings it around and hits the ball off the tee and things like that, but it's too early to really say he's gonna be an athlete."

"Would you like him to be?"

"Oh, of course I would. And I'd be 100 percent behind him. But I'd hate for him, actually, to follow in my footsteps, rather he'd have his own identity than be known as Gary Carter's son. See, I guess, as I was growing up, sports was *always* my choice, and when I lost my mother —she died of leukemia when I was just twelve and she was just thirty-seven—I just knew I wanted to be a professional athlete, that's what I'd set my mind to, and I kept up with it. Though there's been a lot of work involved and it wasn't all fun 'n games, you know, all roses 'n wine, especially catching, 'cause I've had three knee operations, two broken thumbs, three broken ribs, and ligament tears in each ankle."

On my way out, an attendant who'd been standing nearby and had obviously overheard informed me that Carter "was always like that, easy to talk to, friendly, and concerned. For example, he never fails to ask after my wife, who's got cancer, and, long after the rest of the players leave, takes the time to sign every autograph."

# Chapter Eleven

**G**oing into the seventh and final inning, our JV's still coasting along with a 5-0 lead, Geordie's handled eight chances flawlessly in the field, his arm apparently fine. And glancing around at all these parents behind me on the grass, wildly cheering their offspring on, it suddenly hits me how many of them I've known throughout the years of Little League. "They start T-ball so young," Dale Murphy had said. In Chicago, we'd been interviewed on National Public Radio about our trip, and when asked if I thought I'd escaped the pushy-parent trap that plagued nearly half of the athletes I'd talked to, I admitted I was often aware of my own madness, especially when I saw fathers living their lives through their sons and realized how insane it all was. All those crazy Little League games I'd witnessed over the years: managers fistfighting with their own coaches or other managers; fathers yanking their sons off the field by the ear after they'd made an error; mothers flattening other mothers with roundhouse rights in the stands, or, conversely, taking videos of every game their son ever played. "My dad does push a little," Ceo had replied, "but the pushing he does is just enough to get me going. He understands." Though looking at him now trot out to center field for the top of the varsity seventh as Geordie goes jogging out to short, I have to ask myself again: Isn't it enough my being their father without having to be their coach, too?

# Chapter Twelve

On Saturday, we drove back to my hometown of Great Neck, on the North Shore of Long Island, seventeen miles from New York. It had undergone many changes, of course, since the postwar years and sleepy *Happy Days* '50s when I'd grown up there—but no matter, for much of what I saw was clouded forever by memory as I retraced the footsteps of my youth. Toward the first Tudor house of brick and dark wood. Still standing? Yes, but hidden away amid the manicured and groomed, ranch house boom, green, feathery trees that overlapped the road, autumn soon smoking the air with an overflow of scuffly leaves. We used to play stickball on that back lawn with me batting left-handed as Ted Williams and belting them onto the roof, my grandmother serving us grape juice during the breaks—"Dad, you know how many times we've heard these stories?"

Driving on through the town, past the high school I graduated from in 1954. And baseball was one of our links, one of the few areas where my father and I could relate, as he stood before me always in his fedora, Sulka shirt, and black wingtip shoes:

"Did you ever see Babe Ruth play?"

"Naturally I saw him play. 'Bout fifty, a hundred times."

"Was he as good as Williams?"

"Well, one was more spectacular than the other. I mean, of the two of them, the greater hitter, I think, was Williams."

"Did you ever see Honus Wagner?"

"Yup, and Christy Mathewson, Cobb, Ty Cobb, all of them, Tris Speaker, Tinkers to Chance—what's their names, Tinker to Evers to Chance? I saw them play. And Chief Bender, Walter Johnson—I used to go regularly. Because, after all, I remember the Yankees when they played at 156th Street and Broadway, you know, where the hospital is there? Well, that used to be a Yankee ball park. And then what's-his-name, Ruppert, Jake Ruppert, with another fella, Colonel Huston, bought that property there in the Bronx and made it Yankee Stadium."

On we drove, into Kings Point—and here I was, a father now, no longer a son, only father left in my family—toward the home where Ceo was born. A week after my father's funeral, I was sorting out his clothes and the records he kept: of Kennedy's death, Apollo probes, yellowing Yankee programs—and finding those piles of unopened shirts, Egyptian cottons and Sulka silks. What he'd worked for all those years? How many shirts can you wear at one time? But he had to buy more, thirty-five, forty still wrapped in cellophane. And nothing left to buy. So he died. And behind them all my birthday gifts to him, cologne and after-shave sets, odors of the sea, woods, pine, and lime, stacked in the back of the closet—as two-year-old Ceo called "Daddy?" from the door and I turned, kneeling on the floor, to watch him waddle toward me, smiling, his blond hair shining, in my father's huge wingtip shoes, flopping and laughing—both of us laughing—as he stumbled and fell, tumbling into my arms, and I kept hugging him over and over and telling him, swallowing hard, "You can walk in your *own* shoes now!"

That sixty-year-old vine-covered Elizabethan cottage, which I'd rented for $175 a month over twenty years ago, was still there behind the Merchant Marine Academy baseball field as we parked nearby and brought our equipment with us, borrowed mitts, worn softball, and a "Big Daddy" bat, our shadows passing over the green summer grass, and the outline of my hair, a wild ramble, fuzzy-edged and fading. It reminded me of walking to classes at Cornell under the rare sun of Ithaca during finals week and watching the trimmed hedge of my collegiate crew cut precede me. And that morning I'd been trying to brush my receding tangles into some sort of shape, with Geordie, impatient to go as usual, saying, "Dad, your hair looks fine." "No it doesn't, it looks lame." "So? It suits your personality." And I burst out laughing.

We decided on a quick game of fungo, Ceo at the plate, Geordie jogging out to shortstop, and I to center field, adjusting a friend's brand-new, stiff Japanese glove and pounding my fist in the pocket, leaning over into a relaxed crouch, both hands on my knees, and snapping off a blade of grass to set rakishly between my teeth; Geordie ranging far and wide at short, making deep-in-the-hole backhand stops and throws or veering off into left field to pluck those seemingly out-of-reach pop flies from the air; then Ceo whacking the Clincher lazily up into a cloudless sky, where it came floating rapidly down into the sting of my mitt—and onto the grass; next, dropping a fading blooper behind second and looping my weak throw in on a trickle of bounces before setting myself again—as Ceo, swinging from his heels, sent a towering shot rocketing on a high line toward the power alley in right center that had me on my horse, legs churning, racing back, way back, the ball still hanging up there clear against the blue—and that strange feeling as though suddenly shifting into a slow-motion stride, gliding over the grass—and *whap!* reality snapping back with the smack of the ball as I reached out with a last-gasping lunge over my shoulder to snare it in the webbing. Ceo wryly smiling and shaking his head, and Geordie saying, "Wow, Dad finally caught one!"

Yankee Stadium looked like a vast fortified castle with so many guards and Pinkertons around, a stone moat surrounding it, pigeons waddling down the empty aisles, the smell of chestnuts in the brisk Bronx breeze —and, unbelievably, no more terrifying catwalks above! Maybe Steinbrenner had acrophobia, too—for he'd removed them all during that extensive '70s face-lift. The boys sat behind the backstop screen and watched batting practice while I descended toward the Yankee clubhouse, along endless blue passageways and narrow, mazelike turnings to my meeting with Don Mattingly. Slowly I'd come to accept him as the finest player of today, for down in spring training, after all the hoopla, watching him take his BP cuts, I'd been less than impressed. But since then, as I observed him more and more, I began to marvel at his bat control; sudden, jolting power; and, equally striking, Gold Glove prowess at first. Crouching low and gracefully spearing everything within his exceptional range, he played the position more like a shortstop than any first baseman I'd ever seen (and, therefore, I was not surprised when, at the end of the year, he filled in at third). His dominance of the league's offensive statistics was staggering. (He would finish the season with a .422 rush in September and October, leading in hits, doubles, total bases, extra-base hits, and slugging percentage, third in RBIs and runs scored, and second in batting behind Boggs with a career-high .352. His fifty-three doubles surpassed Lou Gehrig's 1927 mark by one, though he admitted never having heard of Gehrig until he came to the Yankees. "Honestly, at one time I thought Babe Ruth was a cartoon character.")

During the past few days, I'd read whatever I could on him: about Kim, his wife of six years and the daughter of his high school football coach; his one-year-old son, Taylor, who was last seen publicly on the pages of the *New York Post* wearing Jim McMahon-style sunglasses and a headband bearing the name STEINBRENNER; how the intensity of his concentration was virtually the same in a 10-1 or a 1-1 game; that every winter he'd hit off a pitching machine at his old high school in Evansville, Indiana, and pretend it was a pitcher trying to get him out with the bases loaded and two down: "For my last fifteen to twenty swings, I imagine I'm in a must-hit situation where a sacrifice fly or a ground ball isn't good enough. I need a line drive. I do it for the last swings at the end of the day when I'm tired"; how Williams, before the start of this season, had persuaded him to be more selective at the plate, especially against left-handers; that he felt when he was prepared, then he could relax and have fun: "I want to improve every day in every facet of the game. I hate to hear that a guy's not a good defensive player. There shouldn't be any bad defensive players, not if they work hard enough. It's as simple as that. There are tons of players who could be a lot better. I'd like to have some of the talent of those guys. Give me their talent and I'll do some *really* big things"; and finally, "I want to be known to my manager as a consistent person, both on and off the field, to never be a problem. I don't want to push by talking. If I lead, I want it to be by setting an example."

The Yankee clubhouse was practically empty, Dave Righetti and Brian Fisher were shooting a yellow Nerf basketball at a toy rim taped to a pillar, playing "Larry Bird." I remembered Mickey Mantle's line "Once you come into that stadium and put the pinstripes on, it does do something to you." And there was Mattingly in the far corner, sifting through a thick stack of mail. We shook hands, his almond eyes and downturned moustache giving him a slightly Oriental look, and he apologized for being pressed for time and could grant me only five minutes at best. He talked with a dark, calm intensity, steady and contained, but always with the impression of a concentrated flame burning inside him.

"What sports did you play in high school?"

"I pitched and played first base in baseball, was a quarterback and all-state defensive back in football, and a quick, white guard in basketball."

"Did your father play sports?"

"I guess he did. But when I was growing up, he was pretty much out of that stage of his life. My father is now in his seventies, so he was more of a spectator then. I was the last child. But my whole family is involved with sports, like my brothers and stuff, so I grew up playin', but my father really wasn't the one who I was watchin'."

"Did he encourage you in any way?"

"Not really. He never pushed, but I don't think there needed to be any encouragement with three older brothers."

The eldest, Jerry, had died at twenty-three in a construction accident when Don was eight. And another brother, Randy, played in the Canadian Football League for five years as a quarterback and punter.

"But never once do I remember my father tellin' me

that you shouldn't do this or shouldn't do that or you didn't run the bases right, or anything really. I just grew up playin' and I learned from coaches, you know."

"Would you like your son to be a ballplayer?"

"To tell you the truth, I just wanna be a parent that can raise my child to be a good person. I want him to be able to make a decision. I want him basically to have the same opportunities that I had, never pushed into sports and never told to play. You know, I've seen fathers yell at kids and fathers yell at coaches, and I don't wanna be like that. I know what I *don't* wanna be like, I'm not sure I know what I wanna be like yet—except I don't want to be a super father or anything, I just want to set a good example."

It was still early, so I made my way to the posh press box, all but barren at that twilight hour. The boys continued to watch BP below as Dan Pasqua lofted a few shots into the lower right-field deck, and my eyes moved up to the façade of the roof far above it, which Mantle had twice astonishingly reached. The second time, in 1963, was the hardest ball he said he'd ever hit—"It was still going up"—and had been projected in flight at between 630 and 700 feet. I recalled the hardest hit I'd ever seen: here in 1948 on a bright, windy day with my father where I watched from behind third base, Ted Williams blast a low line drive off the right field wall, which ricocheted back so fast to the infield on one long hop that he was held to a single.

And suddenly, swallowing hard, all sorts of emotions and memories came flooding back, for *this* was the ball park of my youth: with Williams ripping 'em off the right-field wall; DiMaggio gliding across center with that cool, classic grace; Page hopping the bullpen fence, warm-up jacket slung over his shoulder like a toreador; George Kell's jaw broken with the bases loaded; Boudreau whirling and rifling his throw; Koufax striking out five Yankees in a row; Ned Garver and Ray Scarborough, Dick Wakefield and Roy Cullenbine . . . And my youth behind me now, my father dead these fifteen years, and both of my sons breaking away, going through the same natural adolescent rebellion that I had, moving by me into manhood—but with the memories of this incredible journey to be replayed over and over and over again.

Next day, we drove out to see my old boyhood chum Hal Richman, the inventor of Strat-O-Matic, at his office in Glen Head, Long Island. And Geordie, free to wander and explore this shrine of dice baseball, was in seventh heaven. Hal and I had grown up in Great Neck together, using the game he'd created as a shelter from our shyness, parents, and the pressures of adolescence. Over the years, it had far outdistanced its competitors, gained renown (during the National League Championship Series that fall, Lenny Dykstra would say, "The last time I hit a home run in the bottom of the ninth inning was in Strat-O-Matic"), and made Hal a wealthy man. He lived in nearby Port Washington with his wife, Sheila, sixteen-year-old son, Adam, and seventeen-year-old daughter, Ann (who'd soon be joining John Henry Williams at Bates College in Maine).

"When did you first develop the game?"

"When I was eleven years old. And of course we all loved athletics, but I was no more than an average athlete. Even with all the hours I put in, I couldn't hit a curve ball, I couldn't hit a fast ball, I couldn't run, I couldn't do any of those things. Oh, I could go after a flyball, I was an excellent ballhawk—but that's all I could really do. And that wasn't enough. So the game came about as a sort of substitute prior to camp one summer, Camp Winaukee in New Hampshire. There was only one game on the market then, All-Star Baseball, and it had discs for each player and you'd spin to see the result. And being mathematically inclined, I kept all the averages, and the averages were way off. I mean, Harry Heilmann was hitting .490—he was a .340 hitter, but not a .490 hitter. So I thought I could do better. And maybe a week before camp, I had no idea what dice probabilities were, but I started rolling them a couple of thousand times to get a feel of it, and from that I developed the beginnings of Strat-O-Matic. But there was no pitching and there was no fielding, just hitting cards. And at camp, we had leagues with other bunkmates. Then later, pitching was put in. But I remember when we were fifteen, one of our bunkmates running a Dice Sex League in competition with us. And it got the counselors very upset and they were going to ban Strat-O-Matic because it was creating a moral problem."

"Dice sex?"

Hal chuckled. "You don't remember. Dice Sex was choosing a girl, then you rolled the dice and you would get so much for each roll, for a kiss, for petting, for whatever. Anyway, when we were sixteen, I changed mine to a card game. You picked a card—for example, an ace—and then you looked at the player's card, and an ace, say, would be a fly-out. And it remained a card game till I was twenty-two, in 1958, when I changed it back to the dice game it is today."

"Well I remember how often we played it, how fanatic we were, league after league—we knew baseball inside and out. You could give me any batting average of any player, just his average, and I could tell you who he was, what position he played, and for what team."

"Right, it was unbelievable."

"For example, 1947, .264? Floyd Baker, third base, Chicago White Sox. 1948, .276? Dick Wakefield, outfield, Detroit. And now Geordie can do it, too. Anyway, did you ever conceive it would be a lifetime's occupation?"

"At one point in college I'd hoped it would be. I never thought it would be very successful, I just hoped it would enable me to make a living, put my kids through college, just the bare essentials."

"Did your father play sports?"

"My father came from a poor section in New York

City, the ghetto, Italians, Irish, and Jews, where they almost never played ball. When they did, I remember him telling me, whoever brought the ball was automatically the pitcher. I don't think they even had gloves, I mean the poverty was incredible, they used to mend their own shoes, there was no bathroom in the house, he was working from the age of six, so there was almost no time for ball."

"Did he encourage you to play?"

"No. He liked to box and lift weights, but there was no encouragement for me to play ball. The only time he ever saw me play ball was at camp."

"Did he encourage you in creating the game?"

"No. And as I got older and became more involved with it, as it became a business, he became very upset, because he had developed an insurance business with his brother, and he'd hoped that I would take his place. He hadn't gone to college, he'd only gone through the sixth or eighth grade, and he hoped that I, with my college background, would add quite a bit to the business. So he was very upset that I didn't follow, especially since the first year I lost all my money, the second year I lost all my money, the third year I had *no* money! So I went to my father and I made a deal with him. I said lend me $5,000 and, based on what happens, I will either continue my business or go into your insurance business."

"And what if the game had failed?"

"Well, psychologically it would've been very difficult to work with my father and his brother—they were known as the Battling Brothers of John Street—and I was just not cut out for selling insurance."

"Was he critical of you as an athlete?"

"He wasn't concerned with me as an athlete. He was concerned with me being physically strong, which he was. He was a very powerful man; I was not. I didn't go in for weight-lifting, muscle-building, boxing, which he did. And, in fact, I've only had one fight in my whole life and he caused it. I was nine years old and there was a boy in the neighborhood I didn't like, who was ten, and my father got me out there to fight him. Actually, it was a good thing, because the kid had been picking on me, and we fought. The kid won the fight; I got a couple of good shots in. But my father was cheering and he really enjoyed that."

"How about the game itself? Was he critical of that?"

" 'Waste of time, not studying.' But, of course, it kept me occupied. But he looked at things from a ghetto viewpoint, and, therefore, he made things very difficult at home. He was really like a first sergeant. Physically it was acceptable, if a child did not behave, to be hit."

"So Strat-O-Matic became your defense system?"

"Yes, the game was a great escape for me, from the household and the tension at home."

"Did you encourage your son to play sports?"

"Well, I was Adam's coach from the time he was six to ten, and I coached his baseball teams, his basketball teams. He did not, does not, have any athletic ability. And I think he played, to a certain extent, to please me.

DICK WIMMER

Not being a good athlete, it was very difficult for him. And I understood that, and it really came to a head when we went back to my old camp, Winaukee. There we were, surrounded by all the ball fields, and he looked at me and he said, 'Dad, this was a great place for you, but it's not for me.' And that was it: At ten years old, he retired."

"Did your father ever try to interfere with his upbringing?"

"No, not in terms of athletics—though my father now is a baseball fan, which is interesting, and he's now very proud of my success."

"The game was accepted to the Hall of Fame in 1981. You've had, as you say, success beyond your wildest dreams. How has your son responded to this?"

"Well, I think he's proud of my success. He doesn't play Strat-O-Matic Baseball, I must say. I tried to play it with him a few times, but he's just not interested in sports. His strength is in other areas."

Off we drove to Boston next day, a city where green means go and yellow means go a little faster, and ran smack into the world's greatest traffic jam as we lost and found and lost our way from Cheers to Beacon Hill and Harvard Square till, at long last, we finally arrived three hours early at Fenway Park, grassy and snug in the summer sun. It was here that Teddy Ballgame had banged out his legend, hitting a high of .436 in June of '41, and two years ago, at age sixty-five, had shown a flash of that

166

old form by lashing out a single in an old-timers' game. A reporter had asked him after if he thought he could still put one in the seats and he'd replied, "With a good wind and three days of batting practice, I'd bet on me."

Once more the boys weren't allowed onto the field but sat behind home plate watching the Red Sox warm up, while I headed down to their dugout. So similar to Wrigley with its odd angles, manually-operated scoreboard, and natural carpet of grass, Fenway had first installed lights in 1947, the same year advertisements were removed from the left-field wall to create the famous "Green Monster." And now there was Roger Clemens nodding hello, a big, baby-faced kid with his Joe Palooka body, a strapping Plowboy of the Western World; Wade Boggs slamming his bats and helmet into the bat rack after a frustrating session at the plate; Marty Barrett saying he felt good this morning, like he was going to break out of a slump; Bill Buckner, hobbling like someone seen in the corridors of a nursing home, teasingly called "Seabiscuit" by his teammates; and the amiable Johnny Pesky, born John Michael Paveskovich some sixty-six years ago. He and I sat together on the Red Sox bench, talking about Williams. "Never be another like him. Nobody close to him now." The best today, he felt, was Mattingly, not Boggs, "'Cause I like all-around hitters, power and average, and like Williams, he takes that inside pitch on his fists and, rather than pull a long foul home run, with the crowd oohing and aahing, drops it fair down the right-field line."

Tom Seaver, passing by, then told us of the time he was interviewing Williams for TV's *Greatest Sports Legends*. They were out at Ted's old Hoover High School field and, to start the show, Seaver said he'd always wanted to pitch against the greatest hitter of all-time, so he threw him a high, hard one, right across the letters, and Williams, still wearing his safari jacket and long pants, put it out of there, bang, one swing. "It would've been a home run in any park. It was magic. And then they told us there was no film in the camera and would Williams do it again, and he dropped the bat and said, 'No way! I'm no fool. That was it, fellas, you wanna get it on replay, bring in a stand-in.' So nobody ever saw it."

The White Sox had taken the field now, and, looking around, the dugout was empty but for the grizzled and hawk-nosed manager, John McNamara, his coach Joe Morgan, and a smiling, white-haired reporter, who, after introducing himself to me as Ed Bridges, announced he had a quick quiz for us all: to name five Italian ballplayers who hit forty or more homers in a season.

"Joe D, Rocky C, Rico P," began Morgan, then paused.

"Stumped?" asked Bridges.

"Jim Gentile," added McNamara.

"Good. One left."

"Dolf Camilli?"

"Close, but no cigar. Give up?"

McNamara gave up first, and, after Bridges whispered the answer to him, grinned as he trotted toward home plate and said, "You'll never get it, guys."

I gave up next, but Morgan wouldn't quit.

"Walt Dropo?"

"No."

"Tony Conigliaro?"

"No."

"OK, OK, who?"

"Roy Campanella."

"Oh, gees, that's right—I forgot about his Italian father!"

Back in the stands with the boys, I gave them the quiz, then told them how the Red Sox had nearly signed Jackie Robinson in 1945, the first big league team to give blacks a tryout. Robinson was then twenty-six, recently discharged as an Army lieutenant, and earning $400 a month playing shortstop for the Kansas City Monarchs. But he never heard from the Sox again, and shortly thereafter, he met Branch Rickey. "Not for one minute did I believe the Boston tryout was sincere," Robinson later said. "I was just going through the motions." But Joe Cronin, the Red Sox manager at the time, answered that "He wasn't ready for the majors and we would've had to send him down to Triple-A, just as the Dodgers did. We didn't have a Montreal, our longtime top farm was at Louisville, and we couldn't send him *there*. What kind of reception do you think he would've gotten? So we didn't have anywhere to send him."

As for the game itself, Marty Barrett's "good feeling" proved correct as he broke out of his slump with a bang in the bottom of the first by blasting a Floyd Bannister fast ball high over the "Green Monster" on his way to a three-for-four night and a 9-0 Red Sox win; Wade Boggs, drawing a *chai* in the dirt to wish himself good luck and good health before stepping in the batter's box, went two for two to Ceo's delight, stroking a pair of frozen ropes over short and second base; and the fan beside me, when asked if fights ever broke out at Fenway, answered, "Only when the Yankees are in town." There seemed an inordinate amount of beer drinking going on, much of the brew brought in, and the packed and sprawling concession booths had the noisy reek of an Irish bar as we downed another round of Cokes and recalled memorable games of the past. He'd been here in '49 when a limping Joe D bombed four home runs in three days to sweep the Sox, the last a mammoth shot off the light tower in left, about 80 feet above the field. It was also the night, I added, when brother Dom's batting streak was ended at thirty-four by Joe's shoestring catch on his final turn at bat.

Friday we flew home to L.A. and, as we soared away above rainy Boston, we all agreed we'd like to begin anew—though I still had a handful of interviews to do in California—it was suddenly over so fast. We'd traveled nearly three thousand miles, across eleven states and Canada, taking in games from Wrigley Field to Fenway Park. It had, indeed, been a kid's fantasy come true, as I was the first to admit. But there'd been something more for me.

Still an ardent fan, I'd come to some unexpected, even unsettling conclusions about ballplayers. Rather than the public image of happy-go-lucky, boy-next-door, typical American youth, 40 percent of those I'd interviewed had absent fathers, and another 40 percent had demanding fathers, all but impossible to please. Each player was obsessive in his dedication to the game, for the most part blocking everything else out—wife, family, and friends. And finally, while my sons' hero worship had remained essentially intact, how ironic it was during this trip, when they were going through that perfectly healthy (yet often maddening) rebellion of adolescence, what became increasingly clear was their heroes' *lack* of rebellion: ballplayers still striving to satisfy their real fathers or surrogate fathers in the form of managers or coaches. How many coaches, how many managers had they tried to please since they'd begun, and now well into their thirties and forties, and who'd told them what to do or else?

But then I wondered: Was I any different?

Maybe. Or maybe not.

It was a subject I'd discussed with Dale Murphy but wanted to explore a bit more, so I determined to include a few managers in the remaining interviews I did.

# Chapter Thirteen

**H**igh fives all around as Geordie's game ends with a 5-0 Calabasas win. But just as we begin gathering up all the equipment, there's a loud crack of the bat from the varsity field, and glancing about, I spot an Agoura batter digging for first as his line drive goes soaring toward the power alley in left center—a sure triple if it gets by, to break a 1-1 tie—Ceo racing for the gap at full speed, his feet suddenly sliding out from under him, landing on his knees, bouncing up, and running on before taking off with a headlong dive, his mitt across his body—and spearing it in the top of webbing as he goes skidding over the grass to an outburst of shouting and cheers.

And so strange to realize, after a sigh, that it's my son out there!

# Chapter Fourteen

naheim Stadium in early September seemed like an oasis in the smog as I sat in the Baltimore clubhouse with Earl Weaver. A salty, crusty, and basically sad bantam hen of a man, he'd come out of a two-year, eight-month retirement the previous season, after an extremely successful career, to manage the Orioles again. But now his team was floundering, baseball seemed a burden, and he'd finish the campaign last in the American League East, losing eighty-nine games.

He spoke about his father, who hadn't played sports at all, but had encouraged him. "He used to take me out to the park, we'd get a buncha kids together, he'd do the pitching for both sides, and then when we got into amateur league, or Cory League in St. Louis at that time, the kids asked him to be the manager of the club, and he did."

"Was he critical of you in any way?"

"Yeah, he was critical of me! I never made the major leagues. I tried as hard as I could and I wasn't good enough. Then I became a manager, and every decision I made was wrong—so go figure it."

"Did your son play ball?"

"He was Amateur Schoker-Athlete in St. Louis—I

forget the year—and went on to William Jewell, played two years there, but then gave it up."

"Did you ever hear your father's voice in yours as you raised your son?"

"No, not necessarily, no—in fact, I'm a divorced parent. I spent as much time with him as I could, but it's not like being at home all the time. And this is a different business anyway. When I was married, I was away from home ten months a year managing, so it was tough on the kids."

"Were you disappointed he didn't follow you into sports?"

"Well, I have one son and three daughters, and no, I'm not disappointed 'cause they're all successful at what they do."

"How would you like to be remembered as a father?"

"As a father? That's a tough question. And the reason is because at this stage of the life, you wish you would never have gotten—no, I don't wanna say that either, or I'll get divorced again! But naturally a divorced father always wishes that he would've had more time to spend with his children, not just his son, but daughters also. And that's why I retired, that's why I had the two and a half years off, so I could go visit 'em in their houses, in their cities, and spend some leisure time with 'em. It's a regretful period of my life, but there's nothin' I could do about it, I hadda go on livin'."

"During your years of managing, have you found ballplayers using you as a surrogate father?"

"No, in no manner, shape, or form. I don't talk to 'em, I don't talk to any of 'em much."

"Are there players who are easier for you to handle, and why?"

"They don't need instruction, you don't needa talk to 'em. Frank Robinson I didn't say ten words to in five years. I don't say nothin' to Eddie Murray, very little to Ripken."

"Why are some players problems?"

"Well, they're late gettin' to the park, they make mistakes out on the field, they don't wanna admit their mistakes, they can't understand why you're talkin' to them and not talkin' to somebody else all the time. When you hear the words 'Why me?,' it's funny. To me it's funny."

"Do you think players ever use managers as substitute fathers?"

"No, that's a lotta shit, that's just a lotta shit. I don't see it. Baseball's just a business."

I continued across to the Angels' clubhouse and on up into the dugout. The boys were seated behind home plate watching the Orioles taking batting practice, shagging flies, hitting fungoes as I looked around for the Ripkens. And I smiled as I saw Cal, Sr., standing beside the batting cage and rapping slow ground balls solely out to his son at short that he'd flawlessly field and then toss back on one long hop to his father. Nobody seemed to pay any heed to this ongoing routine, number 7 hitting to number 8, the return throws perfect every time, the father's easy swing and the ball skipping out in the blue twilight air. But to me it was mesmerizing, and a thrill shuddered across my chest!—for here in a marvelous, almost slow-motion moment was the heart of the game, a father hitting to his son, over and over and over again.

Reggie Jackson's muscular strides took him swiftly past me down the dugout steps, and I followed him back into the clubhouse. Besides his testy, aggressive image that gave me pause, he was then going through a four-for-thirty-eight slump, and his .246 average was the lowest it had been that season. He stripped off his shirt to reveal a thick, weight lifter's body, and glowered when I asked for an interview. But then, contrary to expectations, I encountered a bright and sensitive man, thin-skinned but thoughtful, too, once he dropped that defensive shield.

I asked him if his father played sports, and, after a sullen pause, glancing away, he muttered, "Yeah."

"What did he play?"

"He played baseball in the Negro leagues."

"The National or American?"

And he snapped, "I said he played baseball in the Negro leagues!"

"But weren't there two leagues in those days? Because I spoke to Roy Campanella and he told me—"

"My father played for the Bacharach Giants."

"Did he encourage you to play?"

"When I was just a baby, probably five, six years old."

"Was he critical of you in any way?"

"No. Always just, 'Go hard, go hard, humm, baby, go hard.' That's all my father ever preached to me, 'Go hard.'"

"Have you always been close?"

"Yeah, we got real close the last ten years."

"Anything bring that about?"

"I grew up, got older, and realized what a parent is."

"What is a parent?"

"It's the greatest love that anyone could have for you, the strongest. My father is a great friend of mine. My father respects me as a man and a professional. But he also respects me as a son, 'cause I treat him like my father and as a guide. I'm forty years old, so I understand that. I'm a good son."

"Was there a moment ten years ago when something changed you?"

"No, not really. I just wanted to let my father know that I really appreciated him. I wanted to make his life full, I want to make his life happy."

"Do you look forward to having sons of your own?"

"I don't know, I don't know." He paused, glancing off.

"Just before we met, I was watching Cal Ripken, Sr., hit ground balls out to his son, and besides giving me a thrill, I thought this is what baseball's all about: your father hitting ground balls to you, my father hitting ground balls to me."

"That's a special thing. I saw it and I had the same thought."

"Do you think baseball was a way of your looking for a substitute father? Earl Weaver denied this, saying it was just a business."

"Well I had fatherlike relationships with a lotta my managers. Johnny McNamara was like that to me, Dick Howser was special to me—Earl Weaver was special to me."

"One of the things my teenage sons are going through now, and that I became more aware of on this trip, is a natural adolescent rebellion: for example, my music's lame, my clothes're lame, my haircut's lame—"

"Well that is a helluva haircut!" And he laughed, a broad smile creasing his face. "No, I'm only kidding."

I smiled back. "Looks just about the same as yours. Anyway, do you see ballplayers having a need to be managed, be dependent, follow orders?"

"I follow orders."

"But do you see it as more than a business?"

"It is more than a business, but it's a business most of the time. I think with a guy like me who's been around the game so long, that it's more than a business, that there's a certain appreciation that people in baseball have for me, no matter what I'm doing. I'm not havin' a good year, but there's still positive treatment toward me, and it's special treatment because of my accomplishments, so that transcends the business part of it."

"Any regrets about your life in baseball, things you would've liked to have done?"

"No. Though I wouldn't have minded having a son who'd have seen who I was, a ten- or twelve-year-old son. And I would've maybe liked if my father had seen me play more games. But he's seen me play probably two hundred games, he's seen me hit fifty home runs."

"When it's over, what do you think you'll do?"

"Whatever I feel like doin'."

"You think you'll stay in the game?"

"Yes, but I'll do a lotta things. I'll stay in baseball, but I need to spend some time with my friends first, just do regular things like normal people do, I need it, have a year or two of that."

Saturday morning, Geordie was still fuming that we were going to miss the start of his favorite show, *This Week in Baseball*, but we had an appointment with Jimmy Davis, the father of the then rising but soon to be full-fledged Cincinnati star Eric Davis, at Jimmy's home in south-central L.A. Finally given a chance to play full-time, Eric was hitting with tremendous power and running and fielding with world-class speed. Though basketball had been his favorite sport through most of his adolescence, he'd batted .635 with fifty stolen bases in nineteen games in his senior year at Fremont High, after being initially cut from the team.

We came off the Harbor Freeway, and as we turned

down 66th toward Denver, a black-and-white with its lights flashing was parked sideways on the street, at the end of which staggering men were drinking booze out of brown paper bags, leaning on stripped and abandoned cars or sitting on burnt mattresses. "Dad, what're we doing here?" asked Geordie. We pulled to a stop before a neat, tan, single-story house, walked up the drive, and rang the bell.

Jimmy answered the door, a short, round-faced man with an effervescent warmth and grin, then ushered us in as I introduced him to Ceo and Geordie. "They're your kids, no doubt of it, they're your kids!" he exclaimed. "Same eyes, same smile!"

The small living room was dark, windows drawn to keep it cool, and we could hear Mel Allen's familiar Southern drawl in the nearby den on *This Week in Baseball*. "It's OK, you can go watch," and Geordie hustled off as Jimmy began talking about moving his family from Mississippi to L.A. in 1960, working at a Boys Market grocery chain warehouse in Gardena, and playing roughhouse basketball with his sons since they were small.

"Then Eric started playin' with guys like Byron Scott when he was twelve."

"Do you think he could've made it in the NBA?"

"Oh, no doubt, no doubt in my mind. In fact, that's what I thought he was gonna do."

"When did you first know he was athletic?"

"Very small. He's the youngest of my three children, and I always kept balls around the house, baseballs, basketballs, tennis balls, and I used to dribble the ball in front of them, try to let them take it away from me, and a lotta times Eric'd just *take* it. And I used to tell his mother, I'd say, 'God, that kid took the ball from me and I was really tryin' to keep it away from him!' He was six then. And then when he got able to really play in competition, I used to play with them and against them. I used to take 'em over a friend of mine's house, he had a goal in his backyard, and we all would tangle up, they would take my oldest son and I would take Eric, and then we'd be three-on-three and we'd play rough with 'em, 'cause we *had* to play rough with 'em to survive, they could jump so high!"

"How does it feel to have a son be better than you?"

"You know, sometimes I be lookin' at that kid and he'd surprise me, because I always would challenge him, you know, like in runnin'. I'd get off from work and he'd tell me how fast he was and bet he could take me. And I kinda felt he could beat me, but I didn't want *him* to know it. And he kept sayin', 'Come on, let's go, let's go!' and I'd say, 'No, I'm a little tired right now, wait till tomorrow," and Jimmy grinned and shook his head. "You don't wanna believe it."

"Was this a tough neighborhood to grow up in?"

"It was tough, but it wasn't as tough as it is now. When Eric and his brother was growin' up, the older people was a little better than the parents are today. They would kinda watch 'em, 'cause they played right out in the street here. But I was kind of a strict parent, comin' from a strict home back in the South. And if your grandmother raised you, it have a tendency to grow into you, too. And their mother was that type of parent also, she wanted to know where they were at all times. So the area was bad, but not as bad as it is now."

"If Eric hadn't had his athletic ability, what would he have done?"

"Well, he was pretty smart in school and we had planned for him to go to college. In fact, he turned down full scholarships from Arizona, Arizona State, and other schools."

We then joined Geordie in the tiny den where he was still watching his favorite show. They were running through the great fielding plays of the past week, spectacular sliding catches and backhand stabs and throws by the Cubs' Ryne Sandberg, the Padres' Tony Gwynn. *"And finally,"* drawled Mel, *"Cincinnati's Eric Davis—"* gliding back to the wall, leaping high, and hauling one in, before somersaulting head over heels and holding the ball aloft—Jimmy shooting out his arm and clenching his fist, the boys and I beaming and cheering, and Harry Caray's gravelly voice-over bellowing, *"Holy cow, that might be the greatest play of the year!"*

"Jimmy, what's it like watching your son on TV?"

"Too much, man, too much!" and we all walked out to the car, shook hands, and said good-bye. And driving back, Ceo added, "He's the coolest dad ever!" as I told them the story of Willie Mays and his father, Kitty-Kat. They were playing together on a U.S. Steel team in

Alabama when Willie was sixteen and in left field and his father was thirty-eight and in center, still able to go get them:

> And in the second inning, one of the hitters, a left-handed batter, looped a long, sinking liner to left-center, the wrong field for him, and I heard my father say, "All right, all right, let me take it!" But then I was aware that the ball was sinking and he was too far back, and I knew if I cut in front of him I could handle it, so I did, and caught it off the grass-tops.
>
> And I knew also that I'd shown him up.
>
> And he knew it.
>
> I've never apologized to him for making the play.
>
> He's never apologized to me for trying to call me off.
>
> We both wanted the same thing—to get away from the situation where I had to play side by side in the same outfield with my own father.
>
> Because even the great Kitty-Kat was beginning to slow down, the same as his son will slow down, and the only thing worse than being shown up by youth is being shown up by your own flesh and blood.
>
> Because then you got to pretend you like it.
>
> I think he had four or five years, maybe more, of part-time ball left in his system, my old man,

but he didn't play them. I went with the Barons, and "One in a family is enough!" he'd say happily to anybody who asked, but I'd gone and knocked him out of the one thing he loved and lived for, and he knew it and I knew it. It's great for a man to see his son do something he always wanted to do but couldn't. It's great for a man to see his son want to follow in his father's footsteps.

But don't play in the same outfield together. It's like a father and a son chasing the same girl.

Things will never be the same between you again.

All I had to do was let him have that baseball for himself, out there that twilight in left-center field.

I could have said: "Take it—it's yours!"

But I didn't. And I can't buy it back.

The final interviews were held at Dodger Stadium during the second week of September. The first was a brief visit with Tommy Lasorda, he of the waddling, pear-shaped body, boundless brio, and Dodger blue flowing through his veins, in his clubhouse office crammed with photos and cartoons of the rich and famous, Sinatra most of all, where he granted me a few minutes prior to batting practice. I asked him if he found himself being used as a father figure.

"I try to be a father to them, yeah, because the thing

that I said when I became a manager is that I wanted the parents of all the guys that play for me, no matter where they were from in this great nation of ours, whether in Montana, Pennsylvania, Alabama, Florida, or California, I wanted them to sit in their livin' room and say, 'Hey, we know our son's playin' for a man who's not only concerned at what he does on the field but just as concerned at what he does off the field.' Awright?"

And he launched into another interview.

I followed Bill Russell and Franklin Stubbs up into the dugout, the regulars were now hitting, and Steve Sax was asking a reporter nearby if he knew the difference between Lasorda and the Godfather. The reporter shook his head no. "When you go in to see the Godfather, you only have to kiss his ring." The irrepressible Lasorda reappeared soon after, greeting everybody in the dugout—his narrow eyes darting all about—then suddenly began bawling out Kenny Landreaux. Apparently he was late for BP.

"It's your fuckin' ass!"

"But I saw the schedule and Cresse—"

"Then it's *his* fuckin' ass! I wanna know who did what."

Landreaux suffered another spate of verbal abuse, then took off for the batting cage as Lasorda turned back to the reporters.

"Of all the guys to fuck up! This guy's got a C.P.A. and a Ph.D.—no, really. He's got a C.P.A. *and* a Ph.D.!"

"Well, I knew he went to college—"

"Yeah, C.P.A.: cleaning, pressing, and alterations."

"And Ph.D.?"

"Posthole digger. If you put his brain in a bird, it'd fly backwards!"

And how old was Landreaux? Thirty-one. And still taking these tongue-lashings like a Little Leaguer. How many coaches, how many managers?

Across in the visitors' clubhouse, I paused for a chat with Yogi Berra, now an Astros' coach and a gentle and talkative man. When he'd caught for the Yankees, he'd talk to everybody—the batter, the umpires, the bat boys. "I've heard some people say I was doin' it mainly to rattle the batter. But that ain't so. I felt like talkin': 'How's the wife? The kids? Gettin' in any golf?' Stuff like that." Born in 1925 on The Hill, the Little Italy section of St. Louis, his father a brickyard laborer, Yogi had quit school after the ninth grade to work in a coal yard, on a Coca-Cola truck, and in a shoe factory before becoming a ballplayer in 1943. I asked him about being used as a father figure, and he answered, "Well you have to, I think, today." His three sons had all played professional ball, and according to Dale, whom I'd met in spring training, he hadn't pushed any one of them.

It was so strange to be sitting beside Yogi Berra. For how many times had my father and I seen him nearly forty years ago with his looping, bad-ball swing, homering in the clutch or vaulting chimplike into Don Larsen's arms, and now here he was sixty-one with his wire-rim glasses, and I, still a boy inside, was now fifty with my pad and pen.

That was to be the last interview, but on my way out I decided to talk to Glenn Davis, the young Astros' slugger. I'd read the *Sports Illustrated* article on his traumatic childhood, how his father had left for good when he was seven, and that he'd been beaten every single day by his mother until he was seventeen. All through those teenage years, he'd constantly thought about committing suicide, putting a gun to his head, or running in front of a car.

And now he was a major league star, his wife pregnant with their first child. His father had played ten years of minor league ball for the St. Louis Cardinals and Washington Senators, a power hitter with jangled nerves and a drinking problem, before finally giving up the game. "He was the type of person that couldn't handle pressure," Glenn had said. "He had all the ability, but he wasn't able to deal with failure. I think that's what started the problems between him and my mother."

"Was your father critical of you in any way?"

"No, he was never critical of me at all. He never put pressure on me to play the game, always told me he didn't care what I did, it didn't matter to him, I was still his son, and it didn't matter if I did well or I did bad."

"Has he seen you play?"

"I don't know if he's ever seen me play in the big leagues. He's seen me play in spring training. But the thing I remember about my father was he would always teach me, he *always* was teachin' me, and when we did get to see each other—we didn't get to see each other much—if there was somethin' that I did wrong, he would teach me and he always told me to work, work, work, work, continue to work, but he was never critical or anythin' like that."

"With a baby on the way, do you have any thoughts about how you'd like to be remembered as a father?"

"Well, if I wanna be remembered by that child, I wanna be remembered by that child as his father, not a baseball player. And I want that child to know that I love him no matter what, and that he could come to me anytime, that I'm his father and I'm not an idol or a public figure. When I get to the ball park, I do my job here and do it as well and as best as I can, but when I leave here, I leave, and I leave it here. My father couldn't do that, he couldn't leave the ball game at the park where it belonged, and he took it home with him all the time. And that's probably why a lotta the problems happened. But definitely I know that there's other responsibilities than just this kids' game."

# Chapter Fifteen

eanwhile, in Calabasas, the varsity's still locked in a 1–1 tie as they bat in the bottom of the seventh and final inning. Geordie and I are now watching along the left-field line when, with one out and runners on first and third, Agoura replaces their starting pitcher with Ceo's former Little League buddy Mike Maggoria and his blazing sidearm fast ball. But he promptly issues an intentional pass to load the bases; the strategy being to get the force at home or an inning-ending double play.

Working carefully, Maggoria then goes to a 2–2 count on Dave Anzivino before throwing an off-speed curve —that's drilled on a wicked line—but right at the third baseman, who knocks it down and gets the force at home.

Two out now, bases still loaded, and Ceo coming up, everyone in the crowd, the dugout, standing and chanting, Maggoria's father grinning across at me, Geordie whispering, "Dad, Ceo's gonna win it!" "Could be," I reply, my heart loudly pounding, and his brother digging in with his left-handed, slope-shouldered stance, swishing his Black Magic back and forth, back and forth, trying hard as he can to concentrate amid the deafening roar, and hearing (he'd later say) only Ted Williams' words in his mind, *"Hips in front of hands, face the way you wanna hit the ball, hips in front of hands,"* as Maggoria picks up the sign, spins into the windup, around comes his right arm and in comes the pitch, a fast ball tailing toward the outside corner:

Ceo taking that sudden step, the bat whipping around in a long sweep—and there's the crack "that you never hear without wanting to stand up" as a high drive goes rising deep out toward left field, all of us on our feet, the left fielder going back, back, a way back—and looking up as it sails far over his head!!

Ceo barely able to reach first, hopping straight into the air and shouting, and mobbed by his teammates before he comes down, hysterically hugging and pummeling him, till he finally gains a breath and barrels through to shake Maggoria's hand, then, turning toward me and Geordie, radiant with pride, he shrugs, his raccoon eyes smiling.